Strengthening Relationships

When Our Children Have Special Needs

Nicholas R.M. Martin

Strengthening Relationships: When Our Children Have Special Needs

All marketing and publishing rights guaranteed to and reserved by

FUTURE HORIZONS INC.

721 W. Abram Street
Arlington, Texas 76013
800-489-0727
817-277-0727
817-277-2270 (fax)
E-mail: info@futurehorizons-autism.com
www.FutureHorizons-autism.com

Cataloging in Publications Data is available from the Library of Congress.

ISBN 1-932565-10-8

Table of Contents

Preface v

Introduction viii

Chapter 1   Avoiding Blame 1

Chapter 2   Support and Guidance 17

Chapter 3   Affordable Child Care...29

Chapter 4   Money Matters..39

Chapter 5   Time Alone 49

Chapter 6   Effective Communication 63

Chapter 7   Child Rearing and Discipline...85

Chapter 8   Sex, Affection, and Intimacy 97

Chapter 9   Potentials..107

Appendix 1 A Six-Week Program for Couples...121

Appendix 2 About Divorce..137

Appendix 3 A Workshop for Support Groups 145

Preface

If I were a parent reading this book, I would want to know how it came about and what qualifies the author to be telling me about raising a child with a disability. I would also be wondering whether I should spend my valuable time with this book when there are so many other things I could be doing, and other books I could be reading. My guess is that most people reading a book like this one are doing it for only one reason: they are hoping it will be helpful. They are looking for answers to tough questions and are hoping that a book like this one will somehow point the way forward towards a better life for themselves and their families. If these guesses are right, then we're a good match, because there is only one reason I can see for writing such a book and that is to provide some practical benefit—some techniques that work and some ideas that can make a positive difference.

This book began at a lunch meeting in Arlington, Texas, in June of 2003. As a conflict resolution consultant, I had developed training for school personnel and parents who participate in special education planning conferences, also known as IEP meetings (Individual Education Program). I had been encouraged to contact Wayne Gilpin, President of Future Horizons, Inc., because his company not only publishes books of special education interest but also sponsors workshops. Perhaps Future Horizons would be interested in my training programs. And so we met for lunch.

Wayne Gilpin is not only a successful publisher and conference coordinator, but also an author, seminar leader and himself the parent of a child with special needs. When it comes to self-help materials for parents of "special" children, few people have a better knowledge of what is already in print and available, and what is still needed that could be helpful.

Over lunch, it came up that one area of great interest, and perhaps even urgent need, was a book about the relationships of the parents who are raising children with disabilities. There are already a great many books, articles, support groups, and services that address the parenting of children with autism, Down syndrome, attention deficit disorder, retardation, speech and hearing disorders, visual impairments, and many others. But what of the marriage itself? What is available to help marriages remain strong in the face of the special challenges associated with raising children with disabilities? Wayne felt strongly that a book addressing this important topic was very much needed. I told him I thought I could help with that need.

But what qualifies little ol' me to write such a book? Well, I am a parent. I have to add, however, that my child is "normal" in all the unique ways that children without disabilities generally are. That is certainly no qualification. And I do have a professional background in clinical psychology, with a brief assignment as a student intern at a school for special education (way back in 1974). Again, weak qualifications at best. And I do mediation, facilitation, a lot of staff training, and have written quite a number of books, some published and some not. Big yawn. So when all is said and done, what makes me the right person to write this book? My answer: I listen.

Once it had been agreed that I would develop a book along the lines of helping parents strengthen their relationships, or make the best of things if divorce must occur, then what? I knew from the outset that I, personally, did not have the subject matter expertise to write this book, and that I would need help from the real experts—the parents themselves, those who have "been there" and know what works and what does not. With Wayne Gilpin's help, and the help of many others I had met through my workshops for IEP team participants, I was able to get the opportunity to meet directly and indirectly with a great many parents of children with special needs.

I began reading articles and books, and doing Internet research. I joined online discussion groups and posted requests for information. I bounced ideas with parents, perhaps parents just like you. I developed a couple of structured exercises, presented here in the appendices, and used them as springboards for discussion to get parent support groups thinking, talking, and brainstorming about two key questions: 1) What are the common challenges facing parents of children with disabilities? 2) What recommendations can be made to address those challenges?

Based on what they have told me, what I have read, and what I may have learned from my years as a counselor, student, mediator, and trainer, I present this book to you. And I do so with only one desire: that it may be of practical value.

They say that "the proof's in the pudding." See what you think. See if what follows is helpful. You decide. Before closing, I would like to sincerely thank all those who have made it possible, some in big ways and some in small, for this book to come about. And I especially thank you, my reader, for this opportunity to be a middle man, taking what others have given to me and organizing it in a way that I hope will be helpful to you.

NRMM
Roanoke, Texas
October, 2003

Introduction

To speak in terms of the "common challenges" of raising children with disabilities is to risk the errors that go hand-in-hand with generalizations. It is therefore very important to emphasize from the outset that "children with disabilities" is a phrase that can be very misleading, because these children represent an enormous range of differences—perhaps even more than their similarities!

We simplify for the sake of making vast subjects easier to explore and discuss, and simplification can be helpful and even necessary. But if we forget the real nature of our subject matter, then simplification can quickly become distortion, masking the truth as much as clarifying it. We must therefore remember the differences amid the similarities, and not be confused by the conveniences of our English language that lumps unique and *very different* individuals together under such group headings as "special needs," disabled, typical and atypical, normal and impaired, and so on.

There is a valuable saying that:

Truth is like an orange that can only be eaten in sections.

We are about to take the vast subject of "raising children with disabilities" and explore common challenges along with suggestions to address them. But not all children are the same. The challenges associated with raising a bright, verbal, and capable child with a speech and hearing disorder will be worlds apart from the challenges associated with raising a severely retarded child who is also unable to stand, feed or toilet himself. Similarly, there will be enormous differences between raising a mild-mannered and cooperative child with Down syndrome and a very defiant child with self-mutilating behaviors and seizures.

The disabilities vary in monumental ways. Some are temporary and partly "fixable," others may be lifelong and unlikely to improve. Some disabilities are obvious at all times, others are barely noticeable and only occasionally apparent. Some disabilities originate from known causes and have been thoroughly researched, others remain poorly understood, leaving us to wonder and doubt and to fill in the blanks with our own imaginations.

Of course, the parents raising these "special children" will also differ greatly in ways that can have enormous implications:

> *Is the child being raised by both parents, by one alone, or by a foster parent or guardian?*
>
> *Are the parents both available to the child, or is one (or both) usually away at work some, most, or almost all of the time?*
>
> *Is the child an only child, receiving the full benefit of all family resources, or is the child one of two, three, four, or even more children for whom all resources must be shared?*
>
> *Are the parents well-off financially, or are they of modest or very limited means?*
>
> *Are the parents strong in their own relationship? Are they happy together as a couple? Are they good communicators and good friends?*
>
> *Do the parents have caring and readily available family members to whom they can look for assistance?*

Do the parents live in an urban setting with many services available to assist them, or in a rural community where services are few and at great distances from the home?

Are the parents new to the community and the challenges of raising a child with special needs, or have they been in the community a long time, with years of experience at "learning the ropes?"

What of the parents as unique individuals? Where do they each stand along the spectrum of ideal characteristics that none of us have mastered perfectly but most of us have developed to one extent or another: healthy, intelligent, motivated, cooperative, educated, open-minded, well-adjusted, etc.?

Clearly, "raising children with disabilities" involves so many variables that it can be difficult if not impossible to safely generalize. At the same time, we can keep in mind that these many differences are part of the realities—and part of the puzzles. We can be careful not to be fooled by simplifications, and perhaps agree to not get stuck on the points that do not fit for us personally. Given an understanding of the breadth of our topic and the necessity of approaching it like the orange, in sections, we can explore the common challenges and find some ideas that will be of true benefit for us and our children.

The challenges facing parents of children with special needs are not a mystery. A few books, articles, or a little Internet research, soon bring into focus a handful of recurring themes—those issues and problems that are most frequently expressed and discussed. Despite enormous variation *on an individual basis*, parents are generally challenged in the following areas:

1. **Making peace with the child's disability,** *avoiding the "blame game" and finding ways to feel comfortable, confident and even optimistic about the future.*

2. **Finding enough support and guidance,** *not only for disability-related topics but also for self- and partner-related issues.*

3. **Having enough resources for child care** *so that parents can hold jobs and make a living, attend to their other children and family responsibilities, and find time for themselves and each other.*

4. **Meeting the expenses of the child's disability,** *being able to cover the many additional expenses that are not covered even when the parents have insurance.*

5. **Having time alone** *for themselves and with their partner, so that the special needs of the child are addressed in a manageable way and do not make finding time to relax, have fun and enjoy life very difficult or even impossible.*

6. **Sharing child care and family responsibilities** *in a way that both parents find acceptable, so that a pronounced imbalance doesn't add to the stresses on the marriage or relationship.*

7. **Effective communication between the parents** *regarding all topics of importance—not only the child and household, but also each other's feelings, challenges, dreams and concerns.*

8. **Having similar approach to child rearing and discipline** *so the parents support one another as a cooperative and unified team, and so their children receive the benefit of harmony and consistency.*

9. **Sex, affection, and Intimacy** *are important in keeping this area of marriage strong and healthy, so that it does not suffer as a result of the disability and then become an additional stressor to the partnership.*

10. **Having skills to resolve "bad" feelings** *so that emotional balance is restored and feelings such as grief, depression, loneliness, frustration, or anxiety do not become constant features of their lives.*

These ten common areas of concern will be the subjects of the chapters ahead. Our goal is not just to understand the concerns but, to offer specific suggestions to help readers dealing with the particular challenges on a personal level.

After an exploration of these ten common areas of concern, there will be three appendices. The first presents a few simple exercises parents can do to strengthen their relationship as a couple and/or promote their growth as individuals. The second appendix looks at some of the issues parents face when divorce becomes inevitable, as well as how they can begin anew as a single parent or in a new parenting partnership. The final appendix presents two group exercises that were used with great success in the development of this book, in hopes that other groups might benefit from using them as springboards for sharing and discussion.

Most of the quotes presented in this book are taken from Internet postings, discussion groups and personal emails. I may have taken the liberty of some minor editing of spelling, punctuation or phrasing so as to present the essential meaning without the distractions of formal editing—bracketed insertions, ellipsis points, Latin notations, and so on. Unless the quotes appeared in a published book or article, the names have always been changed to assure confidentiality.

Chapter 1
Avoiding Blame

Whose fault is it? Who is to blame when a child is born with a disability? Who carried the bad gene? Whose family has that sort of thing in their history? It may seem absurd or in poor taste to begin a book with such ridiculous questions, and yet from many sources, the life of a child who is "different" often begins just this way. Often it will be the parents who ask such questions of themselves or each other. At other times, it may be the parents' closest relatives—their siblings, in-laws or their own parents. This process of looking for fault might be called "the blame game." It is so common in the area of raising children with disabilities that it warrants our careful attention. It can also be so hurtful and destructive that we do well to start from this point of departure.

Of course, not all disabilities can be recognized at birth. For many couples, the awareness that their child has a disability may be delayed for months or even years—perhaps until the child "should" start walking, talking, or reading. When this is the case, the blame game will start later. It starts with *awareness* of the disability. It begins with a shattered dream.

I'd like to present a few quotes from parents who have experienced this blaming process:

One of the questions my ex asked when we were given the diagnosis was (I will bring this one to my grave), "When do we get tested? When do we find out which one of us has the bad gene?"

Another example:

Before the diagnosis, for two years our daughter's behavior was so challenging, and her father blamed me. When the doctor told us she was autistic, the first words out of my ex-husband's mouth, "Is it inherited?" (while looking straight at me).

And another:

> *I blamed myself for Brandon's disability and I felt sure others blamed me as well. I just knew that if I hadn't drunk that one alcoholic drink when I was pregnant (even though I didn't even know I was pregnant) that Brandon would have been "normal." Or the fact that George's mother would often say, "Well! He didn't get it from our side of the family." Or my personal favorite from her: "It makes you wonder what you did that was so bad that God punished you with a child like this."*
>
> *Of course, being a new mother, I took all this to heart. Looking back, perhaps that was why I felt like I should try to "fix Brandon" all by myself. Maybe in retrospect, I somehow pushed George out of the picture and maybe discouraged him from helping me find help for Brandon. Bottom line was, "I've messed him up; now I'll fix him."*
>
> *Ooooh, this has stirred up feelings I haven't felt in years. Oddly though, I don't blame myself anymore. I have finally accepted Brandon for the way he is and what caused his disability is of little importance. What is important now is to help him find his place in the world.*

Many Forms and Sources of Blame

As we have seen, the process of blaming can vary in time: at birth, or perhaps months or even years later. It can vary in source: from self, partner, relative or friend. It can also vary in form: genetics, family history, drug or alcohol use, "refrigerator mother," vaccination effects, birth trauma, punishment of God or just "reproductive gambling."

The blaming process can also take the form of one partner attacking the other just for choosing to have another child. If one partner never wanted children, or only wanted a certain number, then the other partner who pushed for having that child (the one who turns out to have a disability) may be blamed for the very decision to have the child in the first place. After all, "We wouldn't have a child with x, y, or z if you had only listened to me when I said 'no'."

An interesting reflection of the blame game is the rejection of the disabled child by one of the parents who decides that "He's *your* son," or "She's *your* daughter." Such a parent may live their entire lives as though they personally had nothing to do with the disabled child, and may take no responsibility for his or her care and upbringing. A noteworthy aspect of such a decision to "disown" the child is that it can have absolutely no basis in fact! That is, there may be no genetic foundation, no family history, no clear distinction between the parents—nothing whatsoever to support the belief that the child is "yours" and not "ours." Of course, this scenario can be greatly intensified when there is some factual basis, but either way, the outcome is the same. Blame hurts. Blame distances. Blame weakens rather than strengthens. Its costs far outweigh any gains.

Why do we do it? What makes the blame game so common? What could we be doing instead?

No Pain, No Blame

Let's start at the beginning. What parent prays for a child with a disability? Most if not all parents await the birth of their new baby with all kinds of hopes, dreams, and great expectations. While these expectations may be tinged with some anxieties, they will generally be based on the assumption of a healthy and "normal" baby. The discovery that the child has a disability (at birth or later) will invariably involve the painful disillusionment that comes when our greatest expectations, those in which we have invested so much of ourselves, are unmet. One parent phrased it this way:

> *I used to talk to my pregnant belly and say, "I'm bringing you into this world, but you have to promise to be healthy and really, really good." The birth was uneventful, but what ensued changed our lives. Paul was born a healthy baby boy. He wasn't diagnosed until he was 21 months old. I'll never forget running out of the doctor's office, clutching my chest in pain, crying so frantically I couldn't see where I was going.*
>
> *I truly do not think that anyone can possibly feel the pain I feel for my son. It's quite selfish to think such a thing, but when you find out your child has a pervasive developmental disorder, nothing else in the world matters. Everything I think about now is global: Will he ever marry? Will he ever live on his own? Will he ever speak? I realize now that my husband shared the same fears.*

To understand "the blame game" and begin to find more productive alternatives, we must start from the realization that blaming is a way we handle the pain of our broken dreams and fears about the future. If we take a little detour into basic psychology, a way forward begins to emerge.

Universal Timelines

A model that can be very helpful in understanding emotions and how to resolve them is the "universal timeline." It portrays a direct relationship between events, thoughts, feelings, actions and consequences. It can be called "universal" because it applies to all people of all cultures throughout history; it is an inherent feature of our human experience and a central part of life on earth.

Simply stated, the universal timeline is a five-point model as follows:

Event:

Something happens.

Mental Response:

We think about that event, in words and in pictures, consciously and sub-consciously, with and without awareness, positively and/or negatively.

Feeling (Emotion):

We respond emotionally based only indirectly on the event itself and, more importantly (and more directly), on the way we are thinking about it.

Behavior:

Emotions always motivate behavior, and our feelings will always press for resolution through some form of action. There is no such thing as "doing nothing" with our feelings, because they are going to go somewhere.

Consequences:

Our behaviors, or actions, always have consequences on three levels—for ourselves (whether we feel better as a result of our behavior), for others (whether other people are comfortable with the form of our self-expression), and for the event or situation that we are facing.

The important implications of this simple yet far-reaching model are twofold. First, individuals will differ greatly in their response to the knowledge that their child has a disability. The differences will lie in the areas of mental response (what they think, perceive, believe, assume and expect about this "event"); and secondly, what they *do* with the feelings that reflect their mental responses. These two (mental response and behavior) can be considered the "power points" on the timeline, because whatever is happening and whatever we feel, we have our greatest power in terms of what we choose to **think** and what we choose to **do**.

Compare for a moment two parents who have learned that their child is mentally retarded. In the short term, they can only be expected to feel the normal pain that must follow such a major event in their lives. But after a reasonable period of healthy grieving, how will the parents begin to shape their own experience? That is, what will they tell themselves? How will they interpret their experience? What will they project about the future? How will they allow this event to influence the rest of their lives?

Self-Talk Alternatives

A term that refers to our inner dialogue is "self-talk"—what we tell ourselves in the silence and privacy of our own minds. Although invisible to the outside and often unaware to our own selves, our inner dialogue is powerful! It shapes our feelings, which then shape our behavior, which then shapes consequences. Small wonder that all major cultures and religions have taught that "we create our individual reality based on the nature of our thinking," or "as a man thinketh in his heart, so is he," or "according to your faith be it done unto you." Given the extreme importance of how we choose *to think* about the events in our lives, we can quickly see how the parents of a child with a disability will shape their own future far more than the disability itself.

Consider the differences between the parents if one parent tells himself, "It is my fault because of the drugs I took in college," while the other parent tells herself, "Others have been through this and found their marriages were strengthened; we can do that, too." One parent says, "Our child will always be a burden to himself and others, and will never live a normal life," while the other says, "He can find his unique place in the world, and 'different' doesn't have to mean 'worse.'" One parent believes, "Life's a bitch and then you die, and here is another proof of that fact," while the other parent has faith that "we are 'never tested beyond our endurance' and will find a way through this with love and with joy."

It is certainly not my place to tell any parents what they should or should not think about their child, nor to minimize the feelings any parents may have. At the same time, it is critically important to understand that:

1. *We have thoughts and feelings, but we are not those thoughts and feelings. We project, hold and "entertain" thoughts, and can choose to change them if we are aware of them and decide they are not helpful to us. Similarly, we experience feelings and we express them in various ways, but we are not those feelings, any more than we are the heat we may feel in the kitchen or the cold that we feel in the snow.*

2. *Negative thoughts promote negative feelings, and positive thoughts promote positive feelings; we therefore benefit a great deal by being very conscious (and careful) about the thoughts and beliefs we choose to hold and accept.*

3. *Given any one feeling, there will always be a variety of behaviors with which we can express that feeling; and some behaviors will lead us to much better consequences than others.*

Many books have been written about the power and value of positive thinking, and the reader is strongly encouraged to seek out such books if interested. With only this brief introduction, let me emphasize that one cannot expect to find peace with a child's disability if one insists on thinking negatively about it. While at first it may be a very challenging process to find reasons to think positively and to strive for acceptance, it is important to begin with the understanding of just how powerful our own thinking is in shaping the way we feel. Even if we don't know how to think positively and find acceptance *at this time*, the very decision to try can make all the difference. The following quote from one parent gives us some wonderful insights into the way two people can view the same situation differently, and her own heartfelt desire will surely serve her well:

> *My husband definitely has dealt with and accepted her diagnosis far better than I have. I was devastated and am better but still dealing. He, on the other hand, felt it as an initial blow and then moved on right away. His outlook is that she is our daughter and he loves her no matter what and is going to do everything he can to accommodate and help her be herself, and that she will be okay and find her niche in the world. That is just the bottom line for him. And no, he is really not in denial or anything like that - he truly is how I described. Personally, I think it is amazing and have no clue how he has come to deal in this way - it still honestly blows me away. I wish I could feel like that.*

Blame as a Behavioral Alternative

Having touched on the relationship of thoughts to events and feelings, let's look more closely now at emotions and how they relate to the blaming process that often accompanies the awareness of a disability. In fact, ultimately, the blame game is nothing more than a behavioral alternative for the expression of feelings, and yet one that has very negative consequences.

To clarify how one feeling can have many possible means of expression, consider a parent who feels devastated after the event of the doctor informing her that her child is deaf. We know there will be a mental response (beliefs, perceptions, assumptions, interpretations, and expectations), and that these mental responses will have a great deal to do with shaping the feelings this parent will experience following the news. But the key question for now is what will she DO with that feeling of devastation? Will she become depressed? Will she drown her sorrows in alcohol? Will she avoid the issue and try to lose herself in her work? Or will she begin to blame herself and/or others? These are among the many possibilities by which she will express her feelings. As motivators of behavior, they will surely go somewhere.

We can map this out and then contrast a few of these behavioral alternatives. The diagram on the next page has been called a "behavior train" because it looks so much like railroad tracks, with the train arriving at very different destinations depending on the turns it takes and the directions it follows. For the purpose of this illustration, let's assume that the disability is real and permanent, so true resolution can only mean finding acceptance and "making peace" with the fact of the disability.

Feeling	Behavior	Consequences
	become depressed	she feels no better
		others may not know, so may feel fine
		acceptance never found
	eat, drink, or take drugs	she may feel better, if only temporarily
		others may be unaware or do this with her
		acceptance never found
devastated	suppress and immerse herself in work	she may feel better
		others may appreciate her work
		marriage usually suffers, true feelings are avoided, acceptance never found
	talk openly seek help	she may feel better
		others will probably feel fine
		acceptance assisted by new learning
	blame self or others	she may feel better and/or worse
		target feels offended and belittled
		marriage suffers, acceptance never found

From comparing these alternatives, it becomes apparent that blaming is a behavior that is an effort at escaping the pain of one's feelings. The degree to which it works may vary with the individual, but there will always be downsides: the people who receive the blame are never likely to be comfortable with it; it will never lead to true and lasting "coming to terms" with the disability; and it may serve to distance the person from his or her family and only add to the hardships faced by the child. One parent said it so well:

> There's a kind of tragic irony to this in that the best possible thing for the child is that their family should stay together, that the child should live in the warm, supportive bosom of a reasonably happy, stable, together family. And yet, the parents' marriage gets shoved to the back burner and gets relegated to the absolutely lowest priority when, quite probably, it should be the highest.

When the parents allow themselves to become stuck in negative thoughts and feelings, in blaming themselves, each other, life and God, yesterday and tomorrow, what progress is being made? How is anyone served and benefited? There are alternatives.

Weaken or Strengthen?

One parent made a commitment that the news of her child's disability would not be allowed to destroy her marriage:

> I am a firm believer that if you already have a weak, unstable marriage, any devastating news will make it topple. But if you have something special, something strong, then the news can possibly weaken it, but not destroy it. Maybe someday strengthen it. "They" (who are "they" anyway?) estimate that up to half of all couples divorce after the diagnosis. We will not be one of those statistics.

While on the subject of divorce and statistics, there is disagreement about the divorce rate for parents raising children with disabilities. It is commonly believed that their divorce rate is much higher than the general population's (about 50%), but not all studies support this belief. Whatever the statistics, however, one can never really predict what will happen in any individual family. Each couple will ultimately shape its own future, according to, more than anything else, what the partners choose to think and do. The kind of commitment described in the previous passage will go a long way to assuring their success.

Recommendations

When many parents at a variety of parent support groups were asked what can be done to help parents avoid the common pitfall of blaming, the following recommendations were made:

1. **Recognize the "blame game" when it happens** *and make an agreement to not allow it to divide you. Instead, commit to working together as a team. Accept shared responsibility even if there IS evidence of one genetic contribution. Don't blame yourself either— avoid "emotional self-mutilation."*

2. **Understand the implications** *and be aware of what happens when one parent is blamed, or when the child is considered the child of only one parent.*

3. **Communicate** *openly about your feelings but in a positive way. Talk with each other and with supportive friends or family. Join support groups. Seek professional help if necessary.*

4. **Sometimes the issue is lack of information** *and a belief that a disorder is contagious, represents a "bad" family background or religious sin. When you don't know the cause, ask the experts who do and can give a logical, reasonable and helpful explanation.*

5. **Maintain a positive attitude.** *The parents who welcome their child, however he or she is, are more likely to avoid this game than those who become negative and judgmental. Recognize that this is a choice.*

6. **Focus on today and tomorrow,** *look forward, not backward, and focus on what can be done.*

Chapter 2
Support and Guidance

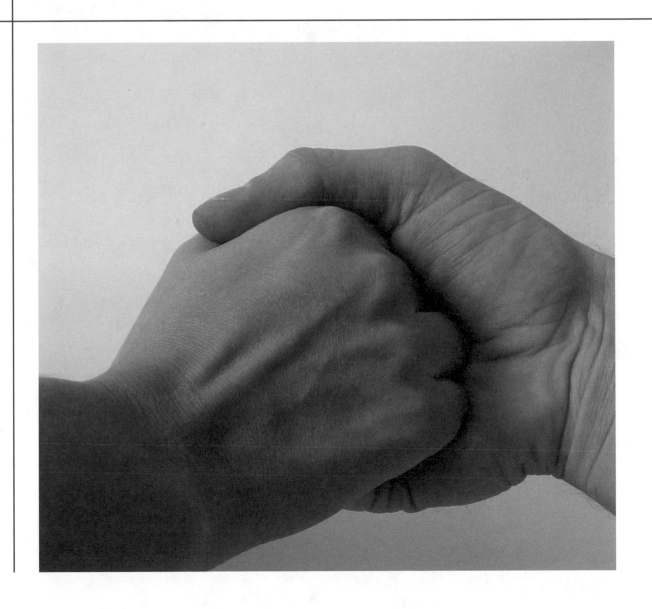

Perhaps the number one, biggest, clearest and loudest recommendation that parents who have raised children with disabilities will make to other parents, especially to the newcomers on the scene, is, "Don't go it alone!" When parents are cast into the role of raising a child with special needs, it is like parachuting into unfamiliar territory. No doubt about it: they're going to need help.

One of the most striking things I am learning from parents is that there is at least one fundamental difference between raising "normal" children and raising those who are not. Our society and culture, our institutions and conveniences—all the things we are surrounded by—are geared towards normalcy. And our society has a fairly standardized and accepted approach to parenting (whether good or bad) in which children are expected to follow the pathways set out by their parents. These expectations may be set directly, according to what the parents say or do, or they may be set indirectly, through the governments, school administrators, and other officials that parents elect. But when children are atypical, *the parents must follow the child!* The less the child conforms to standard patterns, the more challenging it may be for the parents, because each child is unique and will often require "learning as we go."

Thus we hear stories such as "Thomas the Tank Engine" becoming the focus of the family, if only because it is the one thing that captures Danny's imagination and draws him out into joyous expression and contact with the outside world. We hear of a couple that never had a full night's rest until they started running a fan in Tony's room, which almost magically helped him sleep through the night for the very first time. For another, it was dancing with their baby to "The Teddy Bear's Picnic" that quieted the midnight tantrums that otherwise seemed to have no end.

Following the Child

My older son, who is 10, takes a considerable interest in Disney movies, especially "Toy Story." For weeks on end, he would recite the movie from beginning to end. He'd know all the characters, so of course, Mom (me) had to learn them, too. What I did was watch the movie once by myself and compiled some of the sayings from each character. I can remember one time in particular; he was lying in the middle of the mall kicking, screaming, crying - the whole nine yards - just because he could not get something he wanted. So, just out of the blue I said, "Let's go to Pizza Planet," a saying that Andy used with his mom in the Toy Story movie. It was lunch time anyway, and that's what I was trying to do - get him to come with me to get some lunch. He stopped immediately, and replied, "To infinity and beyond! Pizza Planet, here we come!!!"

It is so true that you can't use the same techniques on normal kids as you can with kids with disabilities. To a disabled kid, if they can't find a particular toy, trust me, the whole world STOPS until it is found!!! Your normal kid would just make another choice.

In so many categories of disabilities, the parents will be placed in a similar position of having to learn from the child. They won't have the luxury of being able to just raise their children the way they were raised, nor to expect their children to simply do as we do, listen to what we say, and be like everyone else. Instead, they will have to be inventive, resourceful and creative and let the child be their guide and teacher. One parent phrased it this way:

I think most of us who have children with disabilities are constantly trying to find ways for our children to fit into what society says they should be. But for me, when I quit trying to mold Brandon into what I thought society expected of him and what I wanted him to be, well, it was amazing how easy parenting became. I always thought if Brandon behaved contrary to accepted social standards that I was somewhat of a failure as a parent. It took me years to figure out that was not so.

Benefits of Connecting

As I hear from parents around the country, or read their postings, articles, or books, I find so much pure, yet simple wisdom, so many words of inspiration, so much heartfelt caring and desire to be helpful to others. I learn so much that I now want to share with everyone else. And I ask myself, "How many sleepless nights, how many tears and sorrows, how many anxieties could be softened and comforted if people would only talk to one another and learn from those who have 'been there' before?" Truly there is so much we can learn from each other. How much greater the burdens, frustrations and anxieties when the parents try to do it on their own. The benefits of connecting with those who understand and the risks of isolation can not be overemphasized. A parent said it very well:

> *During that time, we dealt with all of the glaring eyes, with neighbors and relatives thinking we were the worst parents in the world. Everyone had advice: If you would sing to him more ... If you would only read books to him! ... If you just would forbid TV ... If you would stay home instead of working ... If you would just get his sleep on schedule ... Maybe you should get his hearing tested ... No one really understood, and we could not explain it either. It wasn't much fun to visit others, and fewer people came to visit us.*

Whether it is the conscious choice to reach out for help, the recommendation of a doctor, or the requirement of a school, the fact is that parents raising children with disabilities cannot really "go it alone." Instead, they will be forced in a variety of ways to parent in cooperation with others. Whether as a married couple, a dating couple, a divorced couple or a single parent, anyone raising a "special" child will have to parent *in partnership* with others.

Yebbuts

It is perhaps part of the human condition that a part of us will often resist the very thing that we most need and even the very thing we say that we want. The form this often takes is in the "yes, but ..." responses we give when someone offers us good advice. Those "yes, buts" have also been called "yeah, buts," and I like to call them *yebbuts*. It is very important to be aware of them and not allow them to rule us when they stand in the way of what really is best.

When it comes to the topic of "parenting in partnership" and reaching out for assistance and support, there are a number of yebbuts that frequently surface. Some of the most familiar ones are:

1.	*Yebbut, I don't have the time to go to meetings.*
2.	*Yebbut, I can't get anyone to watch the kids.*
3.	*Yebbut, I don't have a computer to visit online groups.*
4.	*Yebbut, my car is not running.*
5.	*Yebbut, the meetings are always in the mornings/afternoons/evenings/ weekends.*
6.	*Yebbut, the meetings are too far away.*
7.	*Yebbut, I don't have the money to go ... to do ... to visit ... to join ...*

When the yebbuts are real, we can approach them as obstacles to overcome. That is, we can find ways to get around them if we choose. To do this, we may have to shift into being "possibility thinkers" and decide to believe that there is a way and that we *will* find it—refusing to believe in "impossible." After all, if others have faced similar challenges and succeeded, surely we can too! So much depends on connecting with others, finding resources for guidance and support, and gaining sound information. We must not let ourselves be painted into corners by the self-limiting voice of the yebbuts. A valuable saying in this regard is:

Argue for your limitations,

And sure enough they're yours.

Support Groups

Just about every known syndrome of disability has some form of support group in nearly every corner of every state. If I were just getting started learning about what is available, I could reach for the "Yellow Pages" and look under Support Groups, Mental Health Centers, or Parenting Assistance and Classes. I could also call any school, pediatrician, or hospital. Just a short phone call to any of these is sure to lead me in the right direction, even if the first place I call isn't it. In other words, getting the ball rolling by making a few phone calls will usually connect us with the people who know what is available in our area, or who else we can call to find out.

One parent phrased it so well when she wrote about the importance of reaching out:

I guess the one piece of advice I could offer to other parents is to be proactive in seeking out ways to help make life easier. In the year and a half since my son was diagnosed, I have found that I have had to make phone calls myself or go online, in order to find the help we needed. It is easy to be overwhelmed and paralyzed into inaction, but the help I have found has been through my own initiative. I feel badly for parents who do not know how to search for help, because often, when parents depend on other people to tell them what to do, the family and child does not get nearly as much help as they need. I have found it helpful to develop relationships with other parents of children with autism. Even though our children vary in terms of the issues they are facing, it is much easier to identify with each other than to try to identify with parents of non-disabled children.

Internet

There is by now a wealth of information, support, and guidance available online. There are articles and discussion groups on every conceivable subject; groups from different cultures, and even countries, sharing in different languages; instant maps (Mapquest, etc.) and driving directions; there is almost anything one could possibly want to know. With a computer and a phone line, the world is truly at one's fingertips. Yebbuts abound with this one and usually include:

1. *"Yebbut, we don't have a computer." (Yebbut, I bet your friends, family, neighbors, schools, churches and libraries do; and older but still very serviceable computers are often readily available at very low prices or even free).*

2. *"Yebbut, we are too old, too busy, and too ornery to learn how to use a computer." (Yebbut, my 80 year-old auntie wasn't afraid to learn, and there are classes, self-help tutorial programs, and friends and neighbors and mentors to help).*

> 3. *"Yebbut, I'm not good with fine motor skills; yebbut, I am not a good speller; yebbut, I have a low frustration tolerance; yebbut, none of my ancestors were computer literate; yebbut, I have fat fingers and they only make skinny keyboards ..." (Yebbut, "where there's a will there's a way.")*

Other Specific Challenges

When it comes to seeking out help and support, three specific challenges that are often heard include:

> 1. *Finding the free time away from our many other responsibilities;*
>
> 2. *Finding child care to cover for us and allow us to do these other things we want or need to do; and*
>
> 3. *Having the support of our partner.*

While these may not be the only "reality pressures," they seem to be very frequently voiced. More importantly, they are often accepted to be decisive. That is, a lack of time, child care, and partner support are often seen as hopeless barriers. They are mentioned now because they can feed all too easily into a vicious cycle that prevents us from getting the very help we most need.

As a hypothetical example, I may recognize the importance of attending the local autism support group that meets 40 miles away on Saturday afternoons. But to attend, I would have to free up four hours—one for driving there, one for driving back, and two for attending the meeting. I have no one to watch my three children while I am away, and I can't just hire a sitter because my child's self-injurious behavior and special dietary requirements cannot be entrusted to just anyone. My husband thinks those meetings are a waste of time and says there's nothing really wrong with our daughter, and he gets really mad if I even bring it up.

How can we possibly find a way through such a complex set of obstacles? These are the subjects of the chapters ahead. For now, let's just summarize the suggestions made by other parents about the importance of getting connected with people in similar shoes.

Recommendations

When parents at support group meetings were asked where parents can go for guidance, information, and support, the following suggestions were made:

1. *Join a support group* right away. Don't go it alone, and don't wait for a crisis before seeking help.

2. *Let it be known that you need help* or have questions. Get out of the house, and seek out help and support from friends and others.

3. *Reach out* to school counselors, pastors and your church community; join Internet discussion groups; call Mental Health and Mental Retardation (MHMR) or other community services; find out what grant-funded services are in your community, such as "Parenting Cottage." Note that specific programs vary from state to state, and even from county to county.

4. *Form a mentoring relationship* with other parents who have been through the same kinds of things, and ask if you can call them when you have a problem or question. Although schools, doctors and agencies will not usually give out the names of such parents, they may be willing to pass your name along to them if you request it.

5. *Get involved in activities* where you can connect with other parents, such as "Special Olympics."

6. *Be proactive:* if there are services that you need, encourage people to get it started—maybe through a church, a parenting group or school volunteers.

7. *Don't let your family become isolated* from other families. If a child doesn't have friends, it is often harder for the family to have friends too. Sometimes parents avoid being involved with friends and family because they are ashamed of their child, or maybe they are afraid of being an imposition on others. They need to get over that—they need to get involved and to know how important it is.

Chapter 3
Affordable Child Care

Two of the most common challenges facing parents of children with special needs are finding spare time and affordable yet competent child care. Obviously, these two are very much related. Without someone to watch the kids, how can we find time for all the other things we need to do? Without time to do other things, how can we connect with other parents, read helpful books, attend support groups, enjoy some quiet time, and so on? Let's approach these two issues, time and child care, as separate topics and begin with the question of child care.

Different Kids, Different Needs

As mentioned in the Introduction, "children with disabilities" is a topic that includes an enormous range of differences. The implications for child care are equally enormous. One child may eat and sleep well, get along well with others, have no significant behavior problems, and therefore almost any baby sitter would do just fine. Although this child might have a speech and hearing disorder or show mild retardation, he or she can be cared for by the same friend, family member, or teen-for-hire as any other child.

The picture changes greatly when the child's needs are more involved. A child who is unable to stand may require baby sitters with the physical strength to lift him or her. A child with epilepsy will require a sitter who not only has the physical strength, but also the expertise to intervene if the child has a seizure. A child who throws tantrums and self-mutilates will also require a level of skills, strength, attention and patience that other children do not. Given that there is such a broad range of differences, let's look now at the options that are available when typical baby sitters just won't do.

Clarifying the Concerns

This issue of finding child care providers has several aspects. Sometimes there are enough available helpers, but we have doubts about their appropriateness. As one parent wrote:

> *Most of the folks that offer to keep them are ones I wouldn't or don't trust enough. It's not that they would do anything bad, just not watch close enough to suit me.*

Is this parent just being overly protective? Probably not. She probably has some very good reasons for being cautious, and yet what specific concerns does she have? What does she imagine might happen if the children were not watched closely enough? What kind of care *would* constitute watching closely enough? Are these concerns that can somehow be addressed? Once these and similar issues are brought into focus, the parents can begin to determine what baby sitters would best fit the needs of their children—and what level of specialized skill is really required.

Sometimes parents believe that only a highly qualified professional can be entrusted with child care. Because such specialists may be few, in great demand, and perhaps very expensive, the parents may feel stuck and see themselves as having no real options. Sometimes this really is the case, and yet very often there are more options than might at first appear.

Let's imagine that the above parent's worry is that her two sons, being very active and inquisitive, may get into the kitchen appliances or household cleaning chemicals. Perhaps she fears that the children might get electrocuted by putting small objects into the electrical outlets, or burned by hands on a hot stove. Perhaps she pictures her children having to be rushed to the hospital after ingesting hazardous substances from the laundry room. Her "mother's intuition" tells her that her kids require very close supervision—much more so than "normal" children—and that's why she would not trust just any sitter.

What if ...?

Every one of this mother's concerns certainly makes sense. At the same time, however ... If so, then what? What if locks were put on the kitchen and laundry room doors? What if the sitter only watches the children in the living room or on the screened back porch? What if baby-proof plugs were put in all the wall outlets?

Instead, perhaps the parent's concern is that the boys will get into fights—that the older one may take the younger child's toys, which will set him off into tantrums the baby sitter would be unable to handle. If so, then what? What if mom and dad get cell phones so they can be reached whenever necessary while a sitter is with the kids? Or what if one sitter was hired for Joey, and Mike is taken to Grandma's? Or what if two sitters are hired at the same time—one for each of the boys? What if three neighborhood baby sitters were paid for their time to take two hours of training by mom and dad in how to prevent and how to handle Joey's tantrum behaviors? A clever parent did exactly that:

> I have trained people that I trust to baby-sit my son and deal with any issues that may come up. This helps a lot and it allows my husband and me to go out at least one night per month.

The point here is not to advise on the best child care arrangement for any particular family. Rather, it is to encourage parents not to give up too easily, but instead to clarify exactly what their concerns really are so as to point towards possible solutions. Instead of, "It's impossible because ...," we can begin to think in terms of, "It would become possible if ...."

One of the best ways to do this is to become good observers of the pictures we are holding in our minds. What are we imagining or envisioning when we think of leaving our child with a sitter? What do we see happening? In the famous detective stories, Sherlock Holmes once said, "It would cease to be a danger if we could define it." Very often, the process of clearly identifying our fears and concerns leads directly towards finding workable solutions.

Let's Get Real

Some of those who are willing to help with child care may not fully appreciate what is involved:

Recently I expressed needing help and could my mom take him one day after work from like 3-7 every week? She said, "Sure, all you have to do is ask, we are here for you, I would love to have him," etc. Let me tell you how long that lasted: about a month, and she was like, "Oh, he REALLY needs to be constantly supervised, and he really doesn't get this or that," and I'm like NO KIDDING! Now she takes him every once in a while, but mostly she says she can't take him because she has things to do and can't just devote ALL of her attention to him right now and do what ever else she needs to do.

Okay, so where do we go from here? We have a willing sitter, but the challenges are greater than expected. Do we give up in despair and frustration? Do we all walk away mad? What if we, once again, explore exactly what the problem is and what possible solutions there might be. What if ...

> *Mom:*   *He really needs to be supervised*
>
> *Daughter: What would make this easier for you?*
>
> *Mom:*   *He really doesn't get this or that.*
>
> *Daughter: What is it we need for him to get, and how could we help him get it?*
>
> *Mom:*   *I have other things to do?*
>
> *Daughter: Is there a way I can help with those other things?*

Once again, it is very possible (though not guaranteed) that closer inspection will lead to meaningful options. Timing and communication are often the keys.

Timing Can Be Important

At the end of chapter two, the recommendation was made that people should not wait for a crisis in order to get help. Sometimes it's not what we say but *when we say it!* Perhaps the child care arrangement above would have lasted longer than a month if careful assessment was made *before* the challenges reached overwhelming proportions. Instead of waiting until problems abound and feelings are strong, we can do a little "debrief" as a matter of course. Perhaps after every child care session we could ask such questions as: How did it go? Any problems? Anything we can do differently or more effectively next time?

This is not to say that open communication is going to make *every* child and every sitter a perfect match, but it may help preserve a lot of child care arrangements. After all, we know that when it comes to children with special needs, the caretakers must often "follow the child." For this reason, we often don't really know how it is going to work out or what is going to happen when we leave a child with a particular sitter. Grammy's expectations of a quiet, joyful afternoon with Johnny may not be at all what Grammy finds when he gets there, and unmet expectations are a blueprint for disappointment and frustration. Again, don't wait for a crisis; ounces of prevention can be worth pounds of cure.

None of this is intended to discount the reality that sometimes family, friends and neighbors are really *not* the appropriate child care providers. Nor is it to pretend that every challenging circumstance will be fixed simply by closely examining it. Instead, it is only to emphasize that we sometimes see failure as a function of the child or the disability when, instead, it may be more a matter of expectations, communication, prevention or timing. Believing in impossibility can be so destructive and self-limiting; we really do well to reserve the word "can't" for when it really does apply.

Other Child Care Options

Hiring a sitter or leaving the child(ren) with friends or family are, of course, not the only options. Recognizing this important need (and potential obstacle), some support groups provide child care as a service at *all* of their meetings—staffed by salaried and/or volunteer workers. One support group came up with a very creative way to arrange child care:

What we did to accommodate the parents that needed care for their kids was we contacted one of the agencies that provides behavior modification services for our kids at home, and asked if they could provide child care in a separate room at our meeting location. We are meeting in a church at this time, and the therapeutic staff support worker from the agency uses a children's classroom there and does some activities with the children while we parents meet in another room. The autism society group funds the staff support worker to be there, so it's free for the parents. We just ask that they let us know a week ahead if they are going to require child care for that meeting.

There is also a need for child care that is not just connected to group meetings. More and more churches, for example, are recognizing the need for parents of children with disabilities to get time off. The *Keller Citizen* newspaper (Nov. 18, 2003), described a very successful "parents night out" program offered by a local church once a month for four hours. Child care is provided at no charge on a first-come, first-served basis. It is open to both church members and nonmembers, and staffed by carefully screened volunteers with a high ratio of adults to children (at least 1:1). A volunteer doctor or nurse is always present, and local restaurants have donated meals. What a wonderful demonstration of the ability of a community to meet an important need through caring, communication, and cooperation! And what a good model for others to copy if such a service is not available in other communities where it may be needed just as much.

Every one of these child care programs began with someone recognizing the need for such a service and speaking up, connecting with others and then working together to bring a wonderful idea into form. The implications are simple: if it exists, find it; if it doesn't, create it!

Recommendations

When parent support groups were asked what avenues are open when affordable child care is needed, the following recommendations were made:

1. **Leave kids with people they already know** *like friends and family; professional help is expensive and not always what is needed.*

2. **Use the help of an older sibling** *who knows the child's needs and with whom the child feels comfortable; pay or otherwise reward the sibling—make it win-win for everyone.*

3. **Do kids exchange**/*sharing with other parents; or form a "parent coop."*

4. **Use the Yellow Pages:** *some day care centers, for example, specifically advertise that they accept children with special needs.*

5. **MHMR offers "respite care"** *on a sliding-fee scale. Find out what services and resources are available in your community. Make the effort and ask for what you want.*

6. **Some churches provide child care services** *at scheduled times for both members and nonmembers. If your church doesn't have such a program, encourage them to start one.*

7. **Check with the local college or university** *because sometimes they may have students in social work, education, or psychology who can assist with child care, perhaps as part of an internship. If they do not, suggest that they develop such a program as a means of helping the students' educations while providing a valuable service to the community.*

Chapter 4
Money Matters

In the previous chapter, we discussed child care, how important it is, what options may be available, and what services may exist that are free of charge or on a sliding scale. Much of the time, however, child care will cost—whether a few dollars per hour to a neighbor teen, or a whole lot more when a professional specialist is required. And child care is only one of *many* extra expenses that a parent raising a child with a disability will face, either to a greater extent than parents of typical children or in complete contrast to them. It is frequently reported that the added financial burden of a child's disabilities has been a great stressor on marriages. Let's look now at how this may be, and at some suggestions that might assist in this area of common challenge.

Many Contributing Factors

Of course, raising a child with a disability is not the only reason a parent or a couple may have difficulty meeting their financial obligations. After all, a great many parents of *typical* children struggle to make ends meet. We must recall once again that "children with disabilities" is a category term that covers a wide range of differences, and the same goes for the parents. As mentioned in the introduction, parents differ widely in their educational backgrounds and income levels. They can differ in how many children they are supporting; how much assistance they receive from family and friends; and whether they are single parents, a couple with one wage earner, or a couple with two incomes.

There are many *other* questions that also have important implications when it comes to the financial aspects of a disability. Are they parents of a child with very extensive special needs or only a few? Are the requirements of the special needs very costly or do they involve little added expense? Do the parents live in a state that offers strong financial support to parents in their circumstances or in a state providing little or none? Does the diagnosis for the disability fall into a state or federally subsidized category and/or one that is covered by insurance? Do the parents qualify for services based on specified income limitations, or do they earn too much to qualify for the help they require? Do the parents understand the system and know how to take advantage of the funds and services that are available? Do the parents have a strong work ethic or do they do little to advance themselves financially? Are they careful with the resources they have, or are they spending unwisely, quite apart from any issues related to the disability? Do the parents work well together in setting shared priorities and maintaining a workable budget? All of these factors will go into the mix that determines whether finances are a major concern or not. Assuming for the moment that it is a challenging area, let's take a closer look at why that might be.

Special Expenses of Special Needs

Until I went through all the channels to get my son's benefits and services in place, we were paying out of pocket for the expenses and were not reimbursed for anything. A lot of our debt came from waiting for a diagnosis, and then for funding, both federal and state. Even with the diagnosis, medical assistance, and funding there are STILL things that are not covered.

Depending on the individual circumstances, any of the following may be expenses that are necessary, important, or helpful and yet may not be provided free of charge by schools or other agencies, and may not be covered by insurance:

Child and respite care	Doctors visits
Specialists' services	Non-approved professionals
In-home health care	Hospitalization
Experiment treatments	Residential treatment
Medications	Non-prescribed treatments
Medical aids and devices	Special diets and supplements
Non-diagnosed conditions	Non-covered diagnoses
Co-pays and deductibles	Costs exceeding insurance caps
Testing and evaluation	Assistive technology aids
Mobility aids and ramps	Hoists and lifts
Damage repairs	Home modifications: alarms, monitors, locks, etc.
Specialized clothing	Special air and/or water filters
Special detergents and soaps	Transportation expenses
Private Tutoring	Private schools
Entertainment and leisure activities	Specialized summer camps
Lost income from time off work	Interest accruing on debts
Legal expenses	Dispute resolution services

Again, depending on the particular child, only one or two of these categories may be of concern and only on occasion—not enough to really be decisive factors in the family's overall financial status. On the other hand, some children may require assistance in several of these areas on a regular or even constant basis, to such an extent that the family is hard-pressed or even unable to pay their bills. A parent wrote of this concern:

> *The pressure and costs to help these kids had really brought us to moments where divorce was probable. It's easy to get to that point with special needs kids. When experts vehemently disagree on what's best for kids, imagine what happens to parents when you toss in the finances for the treatments.*

The Double-Whammy

If anyone wanted to have more money left over at the end of the month (rather than more month at the end of their money), they have two obvious solutions: raise income and lower expenses. A noteworthy scenario often happens, though, with families raising children with disabilities: in addition to having higher expenses, the parents often feel a need to actually *lower* their incomes! In this regard, many parents have decided to only work part-time so as to be more available for their child or children. Some parents have turned down opportunities for promotion so as to avoid changes in schedules or moving to another town, both of which could be very disruptive to their children and their established network of providers. Many parents have reported what this one parent wrote:

> *The financial impact on our marriage certainly caused a lot of stress. We went down to one salary as I left my career to be a full-time mother.*

Often, the issue of not having suitable day care providers figures into the decision-making, as well.

Uneasy Allies

There is another very important dimension to consider in the area of financial stressors. Whether the parents are working at one job or two (or more), and whether they are in agreement about whether one stays at home full- or part-time, there is also the issue of how allied they are in their spending values and habits.

This autism event has about torn us apart so many times, over disagreements on how to spend the money on the kids, the fact that I had to quit working to care for them, and that my husband has no interest in studying about the kid's issues because he's so worn out from working to support our special needs family.

Like the proverbial row of falling dominoes, there can be many interconnecting factors, and stresses often build when those factors intensify one another. But notice in this last example that the issue is not only the amount of income, but a shared vision of how that income should be spent. This then becomes a matter of values, priorities, and communication, which will be the subjects of our chapters ahead.

Recommendations

When parent support groups were asked what recommendations they would offer with regard to meeting the extra expenses of a child's disabilities, here are some of their suggestions:

1. **Get educated about what is available,** *what rights you have, and what budgets are already in place for the services you need. Make your requests in writing so that appropriate accountability can be shown. Qualify for Social Security [SSI]. Schools may have budgets you don't know about, so be sure to ask. In-home family support services may also be available.*

2. **Call MHMR, Ester Seals, The ARC, or other centers** *for suggestions. Keep looking, because every year things change as new services become available.*

3. **Network with other parents** *to find out what they have learned and what has worked for them.*

4. **Seek out no cost or low cost services** *such as: community counseling services; church services; and colleges, hospitals, and other training schools (such as for dental work by supervised student interns or hair appointments through a school of cosmetology).*

5. **Encourage those who can to establish programs** *where all children are accepted—recommend that day care services be provided by MHMR, schools, churches and social groups. Ask for what you want. Get parents to band together to help each other in this critically important way.*

6. **Find people who know their way around insurance**—*often there are ways we might not have thought of.*

7. **Sometimes one can negotiate with "out of network" providers** *(those not on an insurance "preferred providers" list). In this way, you may find better or more sympathetic doctors and providers.*

8. *Find doctors who know how to play the system* to their patients' advantage and who are more willing to be helpful—with free medications or ways to approach drug companies for donations (perhaps to help the companies gather valuable data).

9. *Be persistent* and expect to be rejected or denied the first time you call, especially with insurance companies. Often they will be more responsive the second or third time. If necessary, ask to talk to a supervisor. Sometimes helping them see the alternatives and how much those would cost them can get them to agree to what you are asking for (for example, if he doesn't have this, he might have to be hospitalized, which would cost the insurance company a whole lot more).

10. *Collaborate in fund-raisers*—maybe a band would do a concert in the park, or a church would hold a silent auction. Check with Shriners, Scottish Rite, Jaycees, Lions Club, and other charitable organizations; see how you can work together in support of worthy causes.

11. *Evaluate what services and therapies are in place* - It may be that not all are necessary or a good use of funds, or that some can be obtained less expensively.

12. *Establish a charitable contribution account* at a bank, where people can donate and it can be tax deductible for them.

Chapter 5
Time Alone

One of the most often reported challenges of parents raising children with special needs is that they never have enough time. This includes finding time for themselves—to read, think, relax, or just enjoy life:

> *My son is considered high-functioning and an easygoing child, so his behavior isn't out of control very often. What takes up most of my time are therapies, doctor visits, research, travel (not recreation but related to my son), plus I am a mom to a little girl (age three), do house work, and go to school at night. My phone starts ringing at 7:30 a.m. and doesn't stop until around 8 or 9 p.m. My life often feels like a whirlwind.*

Sometimes "time alone" becomes just time for other work:

> *Kids like my son have very busy schedules, which include school, outside therapies, home behavior programs, lots of doctors appointments, etc., and the coordination of these things is a part-time job in itself. My daughter attends a friend's home daycare for about eight hours a week to give me some time to take care of things at home and perhaps have time to pursue my own interests. Not surprisingly, this "free time to myself" has turned into me having time to play catch-up, and I have yet to use it for personal time.*

Some parents use "going to work" as their personal time:

> *Shortly before my son was diagnosed, I was hoping to go back to work part-time in order to balance out my life. But as I quickly realized how much work we had to do when we discovered my son's disability, I found that I couldn't accept a regular part-time job. Since then, I have been able to work in my field on a substitute basis a few days a month, and those days I consider to be my "days off!" I am still trying to figure out how to not let my son's condition overtake my entire life.*

This lack of time is not just for self but can also be for other children:

> *I'm afraid my older two children (ages 5 and 7) are simply used to coming after Roger now. I try to do special things with them, share quality*

> *time, but sometimes I'm too drained. They seem to just know this, and they count on each other more. I realized this one morning when I awoke to find my older son making his little sister breakfast. This is not something I would have ever imagined. I always got up and prepared their breakfasts and got them ready for school, but they were slowly taking those responsibilities from me. It saddened me in another way that I can't describe.*

If parents have little time for themselves and their other children, it only follows that they will have trouble finding time for their partners:

> *Our marriage is strong, though this has surely taken a toll in some ways. The biggest I would say is that we don't have much time to pay attention to each other and spend time together. All of our attention and focus is on her and making adjustments so that she is in a good place, therefore trying to prevent more issues. This in turn makes all of our lives better, but time is still lacking for each other.*

Or another:

> *How do we find time together? We don't. This has always been a problem in our marriage. Everything comes before our relationship with each other.*

There is not only the issue of the quantity of time spent together, but of the character of that time. So often, parents report that when time is found to be alone, the focus remains on the child with the disability:

> *It is truly hard to take a respite from being Bobby's mom and dad even for a night. We do try to get out several times a month - even if we have to explain to Bobby that Mom and Dad need some "grown-up" time. Once we do get out, though, it is a struggle to get off the Asperger's train of thought before the waiter brings dessert!*

This lack of both time and *quality time* can frequently be a major feature of a downward spiral in a relationship:

> *Months into Roger's therapy, we realized we barely spoke anymore. If we did, it was about Roger. "Did he take his supplements?" or, "Did he throw up today?" This was our new repertoire. I didn't miss the fun, the banter, the dinners out. I wanted my son well.*

Or another:

> *Besides the grief when your child is diagnosed, you then start to live separate lives. For years, my husband went to weddings, funerals, etc. on his side of the family and I attended those on my side, because one of us had to stay at home with our son. We did shifts. I stayed up until 5 a.m. watching, then if our son hadn't gone to sleep, my husband took over. Then on the nights he does sleep, we are both too tired. One other main thing is communicating, but both of us being tired and on the go all the time, we didn't have the time to talk to each other. All the couples I know that have split up, that was the main cause.*

Needless to say, this issue of time can have powerful and far-reaching effects on every member of the family. Without time, what can any of us do? So often this lack of time becomes a vicious cycle, leading to or compounding additional problems. How then can parents of children with disabilities find a way through this complex issue and best spend the precious time that they have?

The Story of The Woodcutters

There is a story that is often told at motivational seminars about two loggers who are having a friendly competition. It has a message of relevance for all people, in so many aspects of our lives:

> Two woodcutters were trying to see who could cut the most logs in a day. The first got started and kept going and going, as fast as he could, never pausing to rest, or to eat, or for anything at all. Totally committed to winning the competition, he stayed focused only on his work.
>
> The second logger, however, would stop every hour or so and walk off into the woods, where he would sit on a fallen log for a few minutes. Seeing this, the first logger felt sure he would win by a country mile. At the end of the day, however, the two compared the amount of wood they had cut, and to the first logger's great surprise, the second logger had cut more wood!
>
> "How can this be?" the first logger asked. "Every hour, you stopped to rest while I kept working. How could you possibly have cut more wood?"
>
> "Oh, I wasn't resting," the second logger replied. "While you kept working, I was sharpening my saw."

Clearly, parents raising children with disabilities must find ways to "sharpen their saws." Working nonstop all day long may reflect great dedication and the best of intentions, but it may not be the best response to the challenge. Rather than working harder, parents must find ways to "work smarter." That is, they must find ways to juggle their many responsibilities so as to make for efficient use of the limited time that they have. Let's look at some of the ways this can be done.

"Where There's a Will, There's a Way."

When it comes to finding time, as in any area of endeavor, it starts with the desire to do so. In other words, no matter how limited our time is, how busy we truly are, or how hopeless our situation seems to be, the first step out of the dilemma is to want one! Just recognizing how important it is to find time for oneself and for each other can be a powerful motivator for change.

While this simple suggestion to "want time" may seem obvious and may be assumed to fit everyone, let's consider what the opposite would look like. The opposite is not that a parent *doesn't* want time. Rather, the opposite of a strong will to find more time is a willingness to be without it! In other words, the opposite of will is passivity. Thus, our greatest obstacle is often just complacency: being willing to accept the situation as hopeless, being willing to accept defeat, being willing to accept that there is no way out of the maze of "no time." Instead, we can get tough! We can make a firm commitment that, even if the answers aren't immediately obvious, we WILL find a way, we WILL resolve this issue, we WILL "sharpen our saws" and be able to cut more wood in whatever time we have. A curious fact of life is that, whether rich or poor, happy or sad, married or single, healthy or ill, whatever our circumstances, each and every one of us has 24 hours in a day. The greatest differences between people, however, often stem from how we choose to spend those few hours that we have.

Setting Priorities

There is an interesting exercise that involves trying to fit the greatest number of stones in a bucket. If we put all the little ones in first, we may not have room to fit the big ones, but if we put the big ones in first, we can often arrange a lot of little pebbles in the spaces around the rocks. The moral of the story, of course, is that how we set priorities will often determine where we end up.

Indeed, setting priorities is an essential part of effective time management; and what is "time management" but the process of making a pile of activities fit into a given "bucket" of time? Yet this process is more than just stuffing the little around the big: it also involves deciding which "rocks" are worth bothering with. That is, setting priorities involves not just the order of activities, but also deciding what to include at all. One of our group members said it well:

> It's hard to balance everything with a special needs child in the family. It is a lot of work, and sometimes things will run smoothly and sometimes it will be hectic. It's often unpredictable, but you have to make it a point to prioritize what is really important on THAT DAY and take a few minutes for yourself and for the individuals in your family.

It can also help to ease the frustrations and the feeling of being overwhelmed if one narrows one's focus to "right here and right now," as opposed to next week, next month, or next year. Another important point to consider is to prioritize your most worthy causes, because there will never be enough time and energy for *all* of them. Wise advice was offered by a parent:

> One of my son's early childhood intervention teachers gave me the most important advice of all: "Pick your battles." It's been my motto all through this. I pick and choose what to fight my husband, school, and family on. Maybe that's what it is all about! She also said, "If you fight on everything, you'll lose it all. Pick one or two things, master that, then move on."

HALT: Little Things Mean a Lot

Consider how this parent juggles her many responsibilities:

> Sometimes I have to let the answering machine get the phone, take a shower if my kids are napping or before they wake up in the morning, schedule days off once in a blue moon when there are no therapies, school, etc. I also get up early before the kids on some days just to enjoy coffee and a magazine for just a few minutes of peace before my day gets rolling.

Coffee and a magazine for just a few minutes of peace! Not a lot to ask, is it? But what a difference it can make.

Viki Gayhardt, author and mother of two children with special needs, wrote a very meaningful article urging parents to take care of themselves, and pointing to some of the little things that can make for big differences:

> *Be kind and gentle to yourself. Memorize the acronym H*A*L*T: Don't let yourself get too Hungry, Angry, Lonely or Tired. Remember that outside your role as parent, you too are a unique person who needs nurturing in order to thrive. Unfortunately, with few exceptions, that responsibility will also fall upon you to make it happen. Rediscover a lost passion, take a class, or buy yourself some flowers. Also, be vigilant in making time everyday for reflection. It doesn't matter if it's ten minutes or a luxurious hour; use the time to breathe, meditate, journal write, get outdoors, nap or do whatever might quiet your mind and spirit. Allow yourself this self-loving opportunity daily without guilt or interruption. Your child and family will be all the better for it.*
>
> *Autism-Asperger's Digest Magazine*
> *September-October, 2003, page 28*

Similarly, time alone with one's partner doesn't have to mean a great big trip to the Bahamas or an expensive night out:

> *When we get breaks from time to time, him from his job and I from mine, it is a breath of fresh air, no matter how quick.*

Even "doing chores" can be like a holiday if they are done in the spirit of sharing and togetherness:

> *My husband and I are usually busy up until the kids go to bed, and sometimes we have to do chores like dishes and clothes once they are in bed. We do take walks with the kids around the neighborhood, which is soothing to them and it gives us some time to chat.*

Doing Your Share

Needless to say, that spirit of sharing and togetherness is not always present for all couples. High on the list of characteristics of those raising children with special needs is that the additional responsibilities fall primarily on just one of the parents—almost invariably the mother. The "tyranny of time" is thus usually felt more keenly by one partner than the other. I asked a parent about this once, and she said:

> *Is there a comfortable balance in responsibilities?? NOOOO!!! I handle all of my son's medical "business" for the most part alone, along with what I have to do at home on a daily basis. I call it business because I feel like I run a small business from home in a way.*

It may not be surprising that moms carry more of the time demands than dads do. The issue perhaps only accentuates our long-standing cultural value that the mother is the primary caregiver and the father the primary breadwinner. One mother addressed this issue in asking:

> *How come when he watches the kids, he's "baby-sitting," but when I watch the kids, I'm just "being a mom?"*

Of course, in many families, there is no father to "baby-sit." In a single-parent family, an already heavy burden will often be that much greater, especially if that parent has no friends, family, church, or others to help carry the load. But whether single or married, this issue of managing the added responsibilities of a child with a disability is often a big one, and in a number of ways. As always, we can only speak in generalizations because individual circumstances vary so much. At the same time, in many relationships and for many parents the implications are often predictable.

Implications of Inequality

First, the partner who is carrying the extra load will often feel more tired, pressured, and stressed. They may have less energy to give to supporting, listening to, or taking care of the other partner. This can be part of a chain reaction with intensifying feelings of loneliness and neglect, and a widening emotional distance between them. The parents simply aren't there for each other any more.

The partner who carries that lion's share of the responsibilities may also feel resentful over the injustice, as if wondering why *my* life should be so totally consumed with caring for *our* children while your life is so unaffected? In the words of one parent:

> *I would say that the responsibilities put the MOST stress on the marriage. I basically felt and acted as though I was a single parent when I was actually still married. My ex-husband thought that it was MY JOB to handle and deal with the children's needs.*

In addition to feeling a sense of unfairness, such a parent may feel truly overwhelmed and perhaps even hopeless. Small wonder that many parents describe feeling depressed, and this is especially likely when they have few "support systems" and see no way out. In other words, the probability of depression will usually be greatest for those parents who are not connected to support groups, have no family or friends to help them, and receive little if any help from a partner. This help takes many forms:

> *My now ex-husband was very supportive financially but when it came to our daughter, he was not with us emotionally. Sadly, I do believe it caused a lot of the reason we divorced. When it came to teacher/parent conferences I went alone, and his logic said it would not do any good if he went. But what would have helped me would have been just having a soft place to fall when we left the conference. It is very, very hard to walk that road alone.*

There is no law that says that a couple *must* share 50/50 in both child rearing and breadwinning. What is very important, however, is that the couple find an arrangement that works *for them*—one that both can support and feel good about. That is, the issue may be more one of a feeling of fairness than of equal sharing of responsibilities as such. If so, how can they develop a plan that feels fair, except by communicating openly *and effectively*? We will say more about effective communications in our next chapter.

Recommendations

When asked how to handle this major challenge of finding time for themselves and their partners, parents at support group meetings made several helpful suggestions:

1. ***Give yourselves permission*** *to take time out for yourself. Let go of guilt and recognize that you not only deserve to be cared for, but that you really can't take good care of others if your own needs aren't met.*

2. ***Schedule*** *plans for weekly or monthly time together or alone.*

3. ***Have one spouse cover for the other*** *so that each gets some time alone.*

4. ***Make arrangements to meet*** *your partner for lunch, or arrange an hour before or after work—some time that can be cleared for just the two of you. Perhaps an employer would be willing to adjust your work schedule—maybe work 9 to 5 instead of 8 to 4—so you can spend time together.*

5. ***Use coupons for time together*** *(i.e.) good for a hug, good for a back rub, good for an afternoon shopping, good for a movie and dinner, etc.*

6. ***One parent can take the lead*** *and set a good example for the other. When one parent spends all the time learning and reaching out for information, he or she can find ways to share with the other—it doesn't have to be a source of resentment.*

Chapter 6
Effective Communication

We have by now explored the issues of avoiding blame, connecting with support groups, finding child care, managing finances and using time wisely. Would it seem outrageous to say that *all of these* involve communication issues?

Bad Attitudes

As a counselor, facilitator, mediator and trainer, I have come to believe that there are two "common denominators" that surface in almost every human problem: attitude and communication. By attitude, I think of such things as apathy, pessimism, and negativity—especially when one member of a team (or marriage) is unwilling to support the good intentions of the others. Such "bad attitudes" can also (and very often) be within one person—within our very own selves! For example, one part of us may want to make a change, but another part seems to always find ways to block the process. One part of us may be committed to being patient and easygoing, while another tends to get frustrated and even irritable. One part of us may feel confident and optimistic, while another sees only the negative and often feels discouraged. It really is possible to have both a yea- and a naysayer within our own selves; in fact, we usually do!

A very wise person once came up with the saying:

Attitudes are the real disability.

Certainly a negative attitude will make any effort much less pleasant and less likely to succeed. In contrast, history is filled with examples of how positive and committed attitudes have resulted in the most wonderful and unlikely outcomes.

Bad attitudes, whether in others or within ourselves, can definitely be a hindrance. Yet they are not always the impossible barriers they sometimes appear to be. There is one thing that can help to fix them, and that is the other of the two universal themes: communication.

Communication

When attitudes are getting in the way, confronting them head-on and talking about them gives the best chance of resolving this all-important obstruction. After all, if my partner and I are having a difference of opinion, and I see him or her as being obstinate, uncaring or just plain difficult, the "royal road" to getting us on the same page is talking about it. Similarly, if there are two conflicting partners' within my own self, the royal road to resolving *that* conflict is exactly the same: talking about it, clarifying the different perspectives and coming into a shared perspective (even if that talking is privately within the silence of my own mind, and the sharing is among the different "voices" in my own head). This process of clarifying and communicating so as to come into a unified perspective is a great deal of what occurs in the counseling process—whether between partners or within individuals.

Without doubt, the one thread that runs through almost every problem in relationships is communication. It is so important and so very far reaching that those who communicate well usually go far in life, while those who have difficulty communicating usually have problems in *many* aspects of their lives. Communication is like the bridge that connects us, one to another, and it is invariably going to be decisive when it comes to improving our family relationships, friendships, work relationships ... you name it! The gift of gab is a gift indeed. If I could put one thing inside a box, tie a ribbon around it, and give it to you as a present to promote success and happiness in life, it would be good communication.

Let's return for a moment to our starting point: the possibility that all of the challenges we have covered so far can be seen as communication problems. How can that be? How does communication fit in when it comes to avoiding blame, connecting with support groups, finding child care, managing finances and using time wisely? Hopefully, this will soon become clear (if I can communicate the idea).

Definitions

It is often of great value to look to the dictionary for insight and direction, not just for the spelling of words but also for their origins and deeper meaning. Words are really only representations of ideas; they have no meaning at all until we assign one to them! That's why foreign languages are so unintelligible: we have assigned different meanings to the exact same sounds and symbols. Oui, si, ja o nyet?

As we look to Webster's for insight into *communication*, we find that it means "a giving or exchanging of information." We also find that it comes from a Latin word meaning to impart, share, or "make common." But what does all this have to do with raising children with disabilities?

Well, let's see ... First problem: avoiding blame. Answer: communicate one's feelings in more productive ways. Next problem: finding support groups and child care.

Answer: communicate your interest and ask others to communicate what resources they know of. Next issue: managing finances and time. Answer: communicate so as to "make common" a plan of action that is acceptable to both partners (and with all parts of oneself).

Communication as Both Problem and Solution

In working with a great many parents in preparation for this book, I notice (from their recommendations) how frequently they identify communication as an important part of the solution to most problems, and yet how *infrequently* they identify communication as *the source* of the problem. Instead, the problem is often described as depression, isolation, denial, lack of time, lack of support, lack of finances and/or lack of information. While all of these issues are absolutely worthy of respect, it can be monumentally empowering to trace these to their common denominators, which will so often be the very same two we identified earlier: attitude and communication.

> *My husband and I started to drift. He didn't understand how depressed I was getting, and I didn't understand how he couldn't feel the same way. That's the first step toward drifting apart.*

I definitely believe it: that they did not understand each other's feelings and started to drift. But could their lack of understanding have been related to communication? What really *is* the first step toward drifting apart? Is it the disability? Is it the different feelings? Or is it limitations in the way we communicate—communications that somehow fail to strengthen understanding, improve feelings, resolve issues, and maintain togetherness? My firm belief, after many years of working with people in conflict, is that effective communication can usually accomplish great things. It is indeed a key aspect of the solutions to most of our problems; and yet, at the same time, weakness in communication is so often a key aspect in *the development* of our problems.

A Review of Behavior Trains

We will recall from Chapter 1 that there is a universal, five-point timeline that is a constant feature of human experience:

Event—Mental Response—Feeling—Behavior—Consequences

Among the many valuable insights we can take from this simple model is that we have thoughts and feelings, and we perform behaviors, and yet we are not any of those "vehicles" of our experience and expression. Instead, we are that inner self who experiences and expresses through mind, emotions and body; and as we use these vehicles, we begin to "reap what we sow" and shape the individual worlds we live in. In other words, we create our own happiness, prosperity, and success in life very much as a function of how we think and what we do.

We will also recall from Chapter 1 that we can map out our experience in any situation and compare our different options using "behavior trains." Let's do this again, looking at our parents who started to drift when "he didn't understand how depressed I was getting." Because there is so much to consider in this example, let's break it into two parts. We recall that there are two power points in the timeline: mental response and behavior. Let's look first at self-talk alternatives (mental responses) and how the partners shape the way they feel based on how they choose *to think* about the event, more so than the event itself.

Part 1A — Husband's Mental Response

Event	Mental Response	Feeling

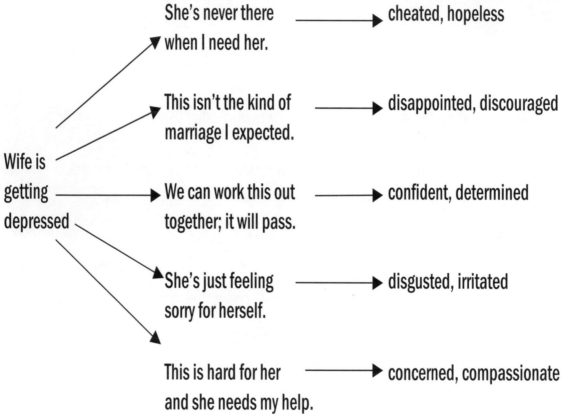

She's never there when I need her. ——→ cheated, hopeless

This isn't the kind of marriage I expected. ——→ disappointed, discouraged

Wife is getting depressed ——→ We can work this out together; it will pass. ——→ confident, determined

She's just feeling sorry for herself. ——→ disgusted, irritated

This is hard for her and she needs my help. ——→ concerned, compassionate

Part 1B — Wife's Mental Response

Event	Mental Response	Feeling

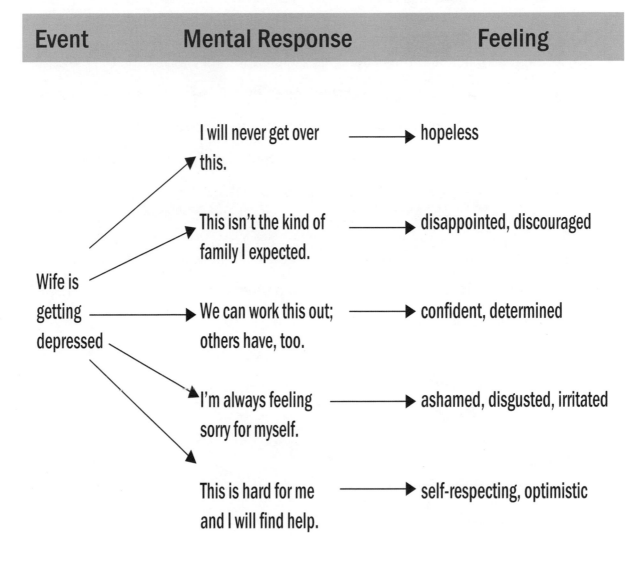

Notes About Mental Responses

The point in the above illustrations is not what the couple should be thinking, but only to clarify that in any situation there will be a broad variety of possible thoughts we might hold in response. And those thoughts are creative: they will shape the feelings that follow. We must recall, however, that most of our mental responses are in imagery and are subconscious—that is, in pictures rather than words and without our awareness until we make an effort to become conscious of them. This process is often much easier with the help of a skilled professional.

Because "mental response" is the first of the two great power points, it is a critical phase in the interaction between these two partners. How they choose to think about their event (the wife's depression) will shape a great deal of what follows, beginning with how they each feel. Note also that we have two "systems" in operation at the same time: two different people generating perhaps very different mental responses to the exact same event.

The next key power point is behavior. We can map out behavior trains for any of their feelings, whether positive or negative, and whether the same or different. For purposes of simplicity, let's assume both partners are feeling hopeless. Feelings are motivators of behavior and will be expressed somehow. So, what will they do with the feelings that they have?

Part 2A — Husband's Behavior

Event	Mental Response	Feeling

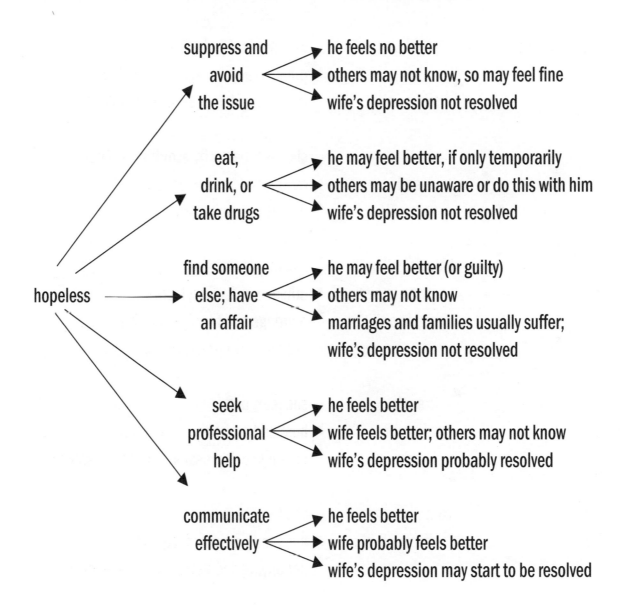

hopeless

suppress and avoid the issue
- he feels no better
- others may not know, so may feel fine
- wife's depression not resolved

eat, drink, or take drugs
- he may feel better, if only temporarily
- others may be unaware or do this with him
- wife's depression not resolved

find someone else; have an affair
- he may feel better (or guilty)
- others may not know
- marriages and families usually suffer; wife's depression not resolved

seek professional help
- he feels better
- wife feels better; others may not know
- wife's depression probably resolved

communicate effectively
- he feels better
- wife probably feels better
- wife's depression may start to be resolved

Part 2B – Wife's Behavior

Event	Mental Response	Feeling

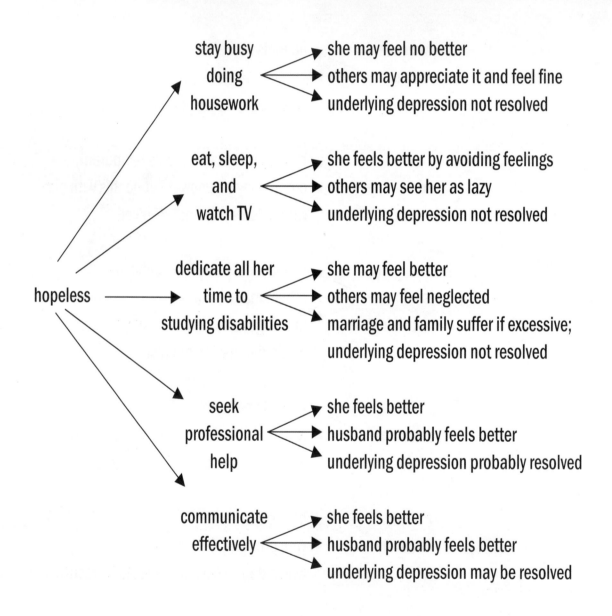

hopeless

stay busy doing housework
→ she may feel no better
→ others may appreciate it and feel fine
→ underlying depression not resolved

eat, sleep, and watch TV
→ she feels better by avoiding feelings
→ others may see her as lazy
→ underlying depression not resolved

dedicate all her time to studying disabilities
→ she may feel better
→ others may feel neglected
→ marriage and family suffer if excessive; underlying depression not resolved

seek professional help
→ she feels better
→ husband probably feels better
→ underlying depression probably resolved

communicate effectively
→ she feels better
→ husband probably feels better
→ underlying depression may be resolved

Notes About Behavioral Alternatives

Just as with mental response alternatives, there is no end to the list of possible behavioral alternatives with which the individuals in our examples might express their feelings. Our personal and "automatic" behavior trains can be called our coping styles or "defense mechanisms," and they are the standard habit patterns (whether good or bad) by which we help ourselves feel better when we feel bad. Obviously, some styles work better than others. That is, they have more favorable consequences. Clearly the best behaviors in our above illustrations are to either communicate effectively or to seek professional help. But if we seek professional help, what are we really going to do there, except learn how to become more aware of our thoughts, feelings, and behavioral alternatives, and get help *communicating them* to each other?

In her autobiographical book, *Fighting for Tony*, Mary Callahan gives rare insight into the decline, destruction and later restoration of a marriage under the stresses of raising a child with special needs. From an exceptional level of self-awareness and self-disclosure, Mary offers many valuable windows into the dynamics of a couple who are in pain and struggling. One quote stands out among many:

> *It began to dawn on me that Rich might have "behaved badly" when Tony was diagnosed merely because he was a human being, and not a TV character. Perhaps he had reacted with anger just because anger was his lifelong crisis reaction pattern, just as denial was mine. Now, in retrospect, it seemed as though it was our defense mechanisms that couldn't live together.*
>
> *Fighting for Tony, page 132*
> *Fireside Books, Simon and Schuster*
> *New York, 1987*

Well then, what options are there when defense mechanisms can't live together?

Effective Communication

As important as communication really is, to *just* communicate is not enough. After all, remaining silent, slamming doors, shouting and swearing, blaming and complaining ... all of these are forms of communication. But they obviously have little to recommend them. We have to look further. We have to understand what constitutes *effective* communication. This has been a favorite subject of mine for almost 30 years, going all the way back to graduate school in clinical psychology, when I was first encouraged to consider how far-reaching a person's communication skills will be (and how much begins to change when they start to improve them).

Over time, I began to see four key aspects to effective communication:

1.	*Hold a Focus (one person and one topic at a time)*
2.	*Talk from the Heart (clearly express feelings and wants)*
3.	*Listen with Respect (listen like a sponge)*
4.	*Maintain the Spirit of Friendship*

Hold a Focus

To hold a focus simply means to allow time for one person to share his or her thoughts and feelings before the other changes the direction. This is a challenge for most people, especially if they have never really studied how to be an effective communicator. Consider this example:

> Jack: *You are always so depressed. You need to lighten up sometimes.*
>
> Jill: *You are always blaming me. If you would just help with the kids for a change, maybe I would have time to get help.*

Maybe it is absolutely true that Jack is always blaming and never helps with the kids. But if this is how Jill responds to him, what is likely to be the outcome? Are either of them likely to feel heard? Are their problems likely to improve? What if instead, Jill held her thoughts for just a moment, and held a focus on Jack's thoughts first. If Jill was willing to hold a focus, she might respond like this:

> Jack: *You are always so depressed. You need to lighten up sometimes.*
>
> Jill: *Say some more about that, Jack. Help me understand what you mean.*

In "holding a spotlight" on Jack's thoughts, Jill shows interest, respect, and openness. It does not necessarily mean that she agrees with him. Once he has had a chance to share *his* thoughts, Jill can then shift the focus and begin to share her perspectives. A helpful way to do this is to simply ask, "May I respond to what you've said?" Holding a focus is nothing more than slowing down and taking turns. Only in this way can both parties have a chance to speak and be heard. It may seem like a small point, but what a difference it makes!

Talk from the Heart

To "talk from the heart" simply means to clearly identify *what we feel* and *what we want*. It may sound so simple, and yet very few people really do this. If we continue with our example of the wife who gets very depressed, it may be that she communicates like this:

> Jack, I feel like this is such a waste. Every day we get more and more bills, and more and more laundry, and more and more yard work, and more and more car repairs, and you're never around to help because you're always working. Either that or you're parked in front of the stupid TV while I have to do all the shopping, get all the groceries, and watch your kids ... I just get sick of it!

Note that although she may give a lot of information, she really didn't clarify what she feels or what she wants. She implied it, perhaps, but only indirectly, and her good intentions may be lost behind her barrage of criticism and negativity. If instead she would talk from the heart, it might sound like this:

> Jack, I **feel** **really discouraged.** I see us falling more and more behind, and I **want** you to spend at least an hour each evening helping me with household chores.

There is a great power that usually goes along with such clear and direct expression of feelings. Note that feelings are always one word (happy, sad, guilty, frustrated, etc). Note also, and in contrast, that "I feel like" and "I feel as if" are always *indirect* expressions of feelings; they really express thoughts and are best followed by asking ourselves the question, "And how *do* I feel when I 'feel as if'...?" Watch what happens when a person clearly and directly expresses their feelings and wants—not in general, but very specifically, right here and now.

Incidentally, people may confuse talking from the heart with being sincere. While sincerity is always very important, the two are not quite the same. A person can be very sincere without necessarily being clear, succinct, and direct in expressing feelings and wants. *These* are what define talking from the heart.

Anger as a Secondary Emotion

It is worth taking a moment to talk about anger. Anger definitely is a feeling, and it is one feeling that we are often more willing to share than others. Yet it differs from our other feelings in a very important way: it always follows *something else* we feel first. Those more "primary" feelings that come before our anger could be any of a great many possibilities, but most of the time they will be one of "the big four": hurt, fear, frustration or injustice. The essential point is that expressing anger usually promotes defensiveness and retaliation rather than understanding and effective problem solving. For this reason, we will usually make much more progress when we talk from the underlying feelings (our hurt, sadness, insecurity, anxiety, overwhelmed, etc.) and reserve anger for when it really is necessary. It rarely is, and when we do express anger, it usually helps to also share what we are feeling behind it.

For example: "I am really angry when I have to do the laundry late at night and get no help from you. [Going beyond it now ...] I feel angry because I feel so overwhelmed. It seems so unfair. I work more hours than you do, and I really want your help in the evening."

Listen with Respect

To listen with respect is to "listen like a sponge." Often, we are so busy formulating our own responses when people are talking to us that we may not really be listening at all. Listening is so important. It communicates many things that strengthen a marriage—or any relationship for that matter. Listening communicates interest, caring, respect and concern. One wonders why we wouldn't all want to do it all the time! And yet so often we don't. As an experiment, try responding to others with supportive and encouraging responses, such as, "How did you feel?" or, "What was that like?" or by simply keeping silent yet giving full attention. Once they get over the shock, they will probably appreciate you just for really hearing them. Whether or not they appreciate you, you will know that you have made a giant step forward in a key element of effective communications.

Maintain the Spirit of Friendship

I have often heard people say something like, "I tried talking to him, but it doesn't help," or, "Whenever we talk about it, it only makes things worse." A curious thing about such statements is that they are usually in the third person: "it" doesn't help or "it" makes things worse (as opposed to "we make things worse" or "I don't help"). Just as third person distances us from our experience, it can also help to "give our power away." So many times that communication doesn't make things better, there is a *different way* to communicate that would give us much better results. Often the central ingredients that are missing are one or more of our four keys, especially the last one, is "maintaining the spirit of friendship."

In this regard, whatever it is we may need to say can be said with venom or with kindness. So often when communications seem to make things worse, it is not what was said but *how it was said*. On closer inspection, it is usually the spirit of friendship that was missing. We can put it back. We can choose to make that all-important spirit a part of our communications. Simply deciding to is often all it takes!

When Communications Fail

A helpful question to ask when talking fails to make things better (or when talking hasn't yet been tried at all), is this:

> *Have I clearly and directly expressed what I feel and what I want with self-respect in the spirit of friendship?*

Most of the time that we have a problem that doesn't get resolved, the probability is very high that the answer to this question is "no." The good news, of course, is that there is more that we can do. We still have power. We still have hope.

Returning to our wife who gets more depressed and the husband who doesn't understand, I wonder what would happen if they spoke, clearly and directly, using the four keys we have just discussed. It may be that their relationship can still fail. It may be that they would need to get outside help—that it may be more than the two can handle on their own. What I feel very sure of, however, is that as soon as they start communicating more effectively, things will start to change for the better—guaranteed.

Before closing this segment, let me say that there is a valuable analogy of the mainspring of a clock: it makes the hands turn and, without it, the clock is absolutely useless. But the mainspring cannot tell you what time it is, because it's on the inside looking out. Similarly, it can be very difficult for a couple to change their relationship "from the inside." The same is true for an individual trying to improve his or her life. Very often, we need the help of someone on the outside who can give us new perspectives and help us develop the skills we need to move forward. So much of personal growth is based on self-awareness, and this can be difficult to achieve on our own. Some exercises will be presented in Appendix 1 to help with raising awareness and improving communication, but don't be afraid to ask for help if a reasonable effort fails to show results.

Recommendations

When couples attending support group meetings were asked how parents can communicate more effectively, these were their suggestions:

1. **Recognize how critically important communication is,** *and make an agreement that you will work on this. Commit to being honest and open, not hiding the negatives or the concerns.*

2. **Seek professional help if necessary.**

3. **Get both parents attending advocacy, educational, and support groups and programs.** *If impossible, then recognize together that the partners are not at the same level of understanding. The more informed partner can set a good example for the other, and the couple can make a date to talk about what was learned.*

4. **Be patient, and sensitive** *to the other partner's feelings and priorities; ask them how best to approach them, when would be a good time to talk and how they want to be kept informed.*

5. **Use "I" statements and a tone of caring,** *as opposed to anger, blame or frustration.*

6. **Set time every day or at least every week to talk** *about how things are going; don't wait for a crisis to start talking.*

7. **Use communication tools and structured exercises** *and see what you can learn or gain from them—like ones offered by counselors, at seminars, or in self-help books.*

8. **Don't let culture limit you.** *Some cultures have strong gender roles and are less supportive of open communication than others. If culture is limiting us, we can choose not to buy into it.*

Chapter 7
Child Rearing and Discipline

Whether with typical children or those with special needs, the importance of both parents being "on the same page" is well accepted. When the parents share a similar view of how to raise their children, it helps to assure clear expectations, consistent responses, and the mutual support that benefits both parents and children alike. At the same time, it reduces the likelihood of the children seeing one parent as the "softie" and the other as the "meanie." It also reduces the likelihood of friction between the parents over who is being too strict or too permissive. A parent offered this perspective:

> *I think that many of the difficulties that parents of young children with autism face are similar to the difficulties that parents of healthy children face - only magnified to a huge degree. I think the need to provide a structured home environment with consistent discipline, lots of 1:1 interaction, etc., is even more imperative when a family member has a disability.*

Of course, this ideal of a unified parenting approach with consistent discipline is not always met. After all, how many people get married with a clear, conscious, *and shared* answer to the question, "What is the best way to raise our children, and what disciplinary measures will we use to manage their behavior?" Even if they had these answers, how many will find their views changing once they have had some experience in the parenting role? Furthermore, whatever expectations they may have had prior to the birth of their children, we know that "special needs" often dictate that the parents follow the child, regardless of any preconceived ideas as to how they intend to parent. A parent wrote on the importance of discipline:

> *These children can't be getting mixed signals. How we were raised as children goes flying out the window. We have to discipline and conform to their needs, or they will be institutionalized or in and out of jail as adults.*

While the potential consequences of "mixed signals" may vary, the importance of conforming to *their individual needs* is a safe generalization. It only stands to reason that both parents working together will be of great benefit to the child—and great benefit to each other. The point was made eloquently by one of our participants:

> If the parents don't have regular communication with a fabulous understanding of each other—what they wish for most and what they feel is most important—you're setting yourself up for a miserable marriage or divorce. It's a hard route to go, not to mention when you feel like the person who should be supporting you more than anyone else in the world doesn't.

A Shared Approach to Child-Rearing

In Chapter 5, we explored "the tyranny of time" that many parents face when raising children with disabilities. We also talked about the common imbalance so often reported when one parent takes on the majority of the extra time demands. In addition to this *quantity* of time issue, there is also a *quality* issue: how the time with their child is spent.

Mary Callahan attributed differences in parenting to a "nurturing instinct" that began even before the birth of their child:

> When I learned that my child was handicapped I was shocked and hurt, but my nurturing instinct was still intact. My wounded cub would need me even more than a normal child ... Rich didn't have a nurturing side to bury his pain in. He hadn't carried the child in his belly. He had spent the pregnancy as a proud and happy outsider. My relationship with Tony had grown with breast-feeding, but Rich was excluded from that, too. He tried to get to know his son by playing with him, but Tony reacted with indifference. Typically in autism, Tony gave negative reinforcement for good parenting, and Rich eventually gave up.
>
> *Fighting for Tony, page 91*

Mary goes on to describe how depressed her husband became and how much this added to the demands on her, while at the same time reducing the emotional support she received when she, too, needed it so much. The result was an amplifying cycle of disappointment, anger, distance and unhappiness. Neither was there for the other.

Differences in child-rearing approaches can indeed become bitter battlegrounds and one of the factors leading ultimately to divorce. A father offered:

> *As far as discipline in our household, I was told by her dad that I spoiled our daughter and that was one reason she had the meltdowns, etc., so therefore, once again, it was my fault.*

Or another; this by a mother:

> *The day Cathy was diagnosed, as we left the doctor's office, my ex-husband said to me, "You think I'm going to believe what he says?" He was so loud with me and screaming that he drew attention to us from others around. I had to take her back for some further tests and he wouldn't go with me. I had to ask my father to go with me. The day I brought Cathy home from the hospital as an infant, he told me the baby will go on HIS schedule - that he would NOT go on hers. I can count the number of times he ever got up with her in the middle of the night; the reply he gave me was, "I have to work in the morning." Both our kids had terrible sleep patterns, which is not uncommon with a lot of disabilities.*

But even when the parents *are* there for each other, and even in stable marriages, there can be great differences in the way they parent:

> *In the first years of Brandon's life, all was well. George pitched in and changed diapers, helped feed him and spent father-son time with him. He adored him. It wasn't until Brandon turned about five or six that I noticed that George began distancing himself from him. By that, I mean we both realized that he hadn't met several of those developmental milestones. Oh, he still spent time with him, but it was almost as if he was afraid to get too close to him emotionally.*

Emotional distancing is a parental response that is often described, especially for fathers, but it is certainly not the only one. Even when both parents remain connected and actively involved, there can be significant differences in perspectives and styles:

> *Of course, there are still disagreements—wouldn't be a marriage without them! He thinks I spoil the boys. Most of the time, I think he lets Tim get away with murder. A lot of times, he just seems lost as to how to handle him. I don't think he truly understands the autism or that Tim DOES have potential and I WILL make sure he has a chance, too. That's a biggie for us. My husband doesn't like me pushing the school, but I feel I'd be cheating Tim if I didn't. He has the potential to make it, so I have to give him the opportunity.*

Differences Can be Good

Mark Twain is quoted as saying it's best if we *don't* all think alike: "It is difference of opinion that makes horse races." No doubt it is a rare marriage (if one exists at all) where both parties agree on everything all the time. But who says that they have to? If we accept there will be differences of opinion, could it be there is something good in that? What would life be like if everywhere we went, we were surrounded ONLY with people who agreed with us? Beyond the momentary bliss, we would probably remain forever stuck at the level of our present knowledge and abilities! We would have little incentive or opportunity for growth. Our horses would have little reason to run. A wise person phrased it this way: "If I only want to hear from people who agree with me, I might as well talk to myself."

But what of our children? How can we handle differences of opinion in the context of a marriage and the context of parenting children with unique and special needs? Can differences be good? Can they even be tolerated? Perhaps the issue is not so much that there are differences, but *what we do* with those differences—how we choose to handle them.

Awareness

In Chapter 3, the fictional detective, Sherlock Holmes, was quoted as saying that "it would cease to be a danger if we could define it." The process of simply identifying our concerns is often a major part of the process of moving forward. But so often we fail to do this, or we give up too easily and neglect to follow through. If a couple is having trouble over the issue of how they are raising their children together, the first step must always be one of becoming conscious of the issue. Only then will they be in a position to do anything different. An old saying says so much:

With awareness comes the ability to make flexible choices.

Are we aware of the importance of having a similar approach? Are we aware of the implications of being at cross-purposes? Are we aware of our thoughts and feelings (our own and the other person's)? Are we aware of how we are expressing our feelings and what some of our better options might be? Once we have such awareness, our challenge will become a matter of the same "dynamic duo" that we discussed in the previous chapter: attitude and communication.

Attitude and Communication

A major part of this process of exploration will, of course, involve communication. We recall from Chapter 6 the four important keys:

1.	*Hold a focus.*
2.	*Talk from the heart.*
3.	*Listen with respect.*
4.	*Maintain the spirit of friendship.*

Some readers may say, "I'll try that!" and find new energy and new hope for coming into a stronger alignment with their husband or wife. Others are likely to hear the voice of the yebbuts we spoke of in Chapter 2: "Yebbut, we tried that and it didn't work; yebbut, she never has time; yebbut, he's always in denial; yebbut, he won't talk; yebbut, she won't listen; yebbut, he don't, she won't, they don't, and we can't ..." The upshot is that nothing changes and the issues remain the same. **Beware the voice of the yebbuts**. A wonderful saying that is not always popular is:

If you always do what you've always done,

You will always get what you always got.

Very often when we remain at odds with our partners, it is not because the situation is as impossible as we sometimes believe. Most of the time, we just have to find the "combination to the lock"—we have to try something different.

Families are interconnected systems, and a change in one member often leads to changes in others. Some parents describe amazing changes when they make a shift within themselves:

> *My husband and I have gone through quite a bit. What helped us the most was a combination of two things: religion and a non-judgmental attitude. Never assume that what anyone does is to annoy you or ruin your life, but assume that all people are trying to do the best they can, based on their understanding, needs, and really what has worked for them in the past (or perhaps it's the only way they know how to behave). If they really are doing the best they can, then there's no reason to be unhappy at anyone. I found that when I had no expectations on my husband, but just enjoyed all the good that he naturally does to help his family, our marriage thrived. I didn't need him to think the same way I do, but I do let him know what I am doing with the kids and let him know exactly what type of support I need.*

Another parent shared a very similar message about attitude:

> *If I could accept certain limitations from my daughter because I love her (although not necessarily all her behaviors), I had to learn to allow my husband to have some of those same limitations. There are things we simply cannot change about our spouses, and we must learn to accept them. We each carry our own baggage and factors. Love and marriage is hard enough for any couple in today's world. For our families, it is a monumental task but brings the greatest rewards. Loving each other and loving ourselves, warts and all, is key to success.*

From a *willingness* to work together, positive attitudes, and healthy communications, so many couples have been able to achieve amazing results. Because so often they will have to "follow the child" and learn as they go, in most cases they are also likely to need a healthy dose of creativity.

Creativity

The creativity that is so often needed may relate to shaping behaviors—rewarding and encouraging desired behaviors while discouraging their opposites. But this need for creativity may also relate to relationship building. As a mother wrote:

> For a while, my husband and I were not on the same page when it came to Robert. Family counseling helped a lot. I am very lucky that my husband is the type of man that loves his son despite the problems. He has confided in me that the diagnosis is a disappointment. The counseling helped us find new goals etc. for our son and showed us how to interact and have fun. One example: family vacations. When we grew up our families took us on historical/education trips - to Yosemite, Grand Canyon, Carlsbad Caverns. We would love to see these things but know it's not good for Robert. We stick to amusement parks and the beach.

Another parent saw her husband take a more active role with their child when he found a common interest:

> I always felt very alone taking care of Arnie until he was about 14 and started bowling with Special Olympics. My husband took him to the bowling alley and got to know the other families and started enjoying Arnie.

The challenges are not always easy, but the rewards of working as a unified team are surely worth the efforts, and it really can be done. A mother who has established a good relationship with her husband offered these thoughts:

> When one has reached their limit, the other takes over. We have always made a point of realizing that and just automatically jumping in and relieving the other. I would say that my husband and I are equal caretakers for him. We both know everything and participate in everything revolving around him. We are a great team. Truthfully, we both have different strengths and it all seems to balance out in the end. We work very hard to make it all work, and it is so worth it.

Recommendations

When parents at support group meetings were asked how parents can work together as a unified team, these were their recommendations:

1. **Communicate openly and honestly,** with love (not blame or anger) in a balanced way. Build time to talk into your life together.

2. **Work together.** Come to a mutual agreement that child rearing will not be just one parent's responsibility.

3. **Make a plan before the event** as to how you want to respond when a situation comes up (not in the moment, when time is short and tensions are high).

4. **Pick your battles.** Allow for differences when they are not of real significance. If important issues cannot be resolved, seek outside help or professional counseling.

5. **Share books, articles, or classes** on parenting—perhaps through community or church.

6. **Don't let the child play one parent against the other.** Prepare for it, recognize when it happens, have a plan for how you will deal with it.

7. **Expect sibling rivalries:** "How come he doesn't have to do this," or "I always have to do that?" Have a unified plan of response in advance.

8. **Support each other's decisions,** and if there is disagreement, talk about it in private (away from kids or other people). Don't let the kids see you as divided, and don't make one parent seem the good guy and the other the bad guy.

Chapter 8
Sex, Affection and Intimacy

As a marriage counselor, I would often have to ask the question, "How's your sex life?" Part of me always felt awkward about asking such a personal question. After all, it really was none of *my* business. At the same time, sex and marriage usually go together, and the answers to this question would often shed light on the health of the relationship in more general terms, as well as point towards areas of conflict that warranted attention.

Sex as an "Indicator"

What I came to understand was that couples who had a mutually satisfying sexual relationship rarely came to my office for help. On the other hand, virtually all who had difficulties with sex had difficulties in other areas as well. Occasionally, sex *was* the problem, but far more often, sex was an indicator—pointing to *other areas* where the couple was having trouble getting along.

A focus on improving their sex life would sometimes result in improvements in a number of other areas. But more often than not, improvement in their sexual relationship was just not likely to happen until other areas were addressed as well—or even first. What those "other areas" were might be obvious: resolving anger and resentments; increasing mutual support and understanding; improving communication; and restoring some of the joy in their togetherness that probably drew them together in the first place.

When relationships begin to weaken, sex is often an early casualty. What happens next is frequently predictable: the absence of a healthy sexual relationship becomes a problem in and of itself. Tensions and hostilities may rise, emotional distance increases, feelings of support and satisfaction diminish, the attraction to other people may increase and the decline of the marriage may be accelerated. An interesting fact about sex is it is one area of marriage where the partners have to be "in sync." If husband likes bowling, but wife prefers golf; if husband likes green beans, but wife prefers tomatoes; if husband likes comedies, but wife prefers soaps … all of these differences can be easily accommodated. But if one partner likes sex and the other doesn't, it's a safe bet this boat is going to rock. It is not always the husband complaining about a lack of interest or response from his wife. Very often, it is the wife who complains that her husband is inattentive and unresponsive. Either prescription can make for misery, and it is a people thing—not a male or female issue.

In talking about sex, we can expand our focus and look at the broader perspective—not just sex, per se, but also intimacy and affection in a general sense. For most couples, these three will go together. After all, it is a rare couple that has a great sex life with no intimacy or affection. It is just as rare will we find an intimate and affectionate couple that is celibate. All three are essential aspects of a satisfying, healthy marriage. They can become particularly challenging when the partners are faced with raising a child with a disability.

Sex Rarely Stands Alone

In some ways, it makes little sense to look at sex, affection, and intimacy as a topic apart from others that we have covered already; certainly there will be overlap and interrelation. The couple stuck in "the blame game" about the birth of a child with a disability is not likely to feel warm and responsive to each other. The wife who resents her husband for not helping with her many added responsibilities will probably find her unresolved anger creeping into the bedroom at night. The husband who believes his wife's permissive approach to child rearing undermines his role in the family may show little affection during the day, and may seem distant when the lights are low—the same with a husband who fears that his wife's unnecessary spending is certain to ruin them both. All of these negative perceptions and unresolved feelings will surely become obstacles to the affection, intimacy, and fulfilling sexual relationship they might both, ideally, hope for. It matters little whether the perceptions are true or not, or only partly so—the feelings and beliefs are very real in any case, and they *will* exert an influence.

Of course, *any* couple can have challenges in the area of sex, affection, and intimacy—this is by no means limited to those raising children with disabilities. And the difficulties can stem from a wide variety of possible sources. At the same time, there are a number of areas where couples raising "special kids" may have special, or at least extra, challenges. These will usually be in the following areas:

1.	*Fatigue*
2.	*Medications*
3.	*Negative thoughts*
4.	*Negative feelings*
5.	*Accommodating the disabilities*

We spoke in Chapter 5 about the many time demands that can be part of the daily life of a couple raising a child with a disability. As one mother wrote:

> *My husband often had to work late with his job, so I would be up with Alicia till one or two in the morning, while he would stay up the rest of the night with her. Our house was a constant nightmare. My husband and I were at our wits' end. We never saw each other, since he needed to sleep whenever we were both home at the same time, to make up for lost sleep taking care of her.*

Beyond the issue of little time together and little time for intimacy, there is also the question of how allied the parents are. Do they share the same values and support one another in the roles that they play, or does one see the other as uncaring, neglectful, or unfair? One mother spoke of her view of unfairness:

> *There is resentment about how the mom is always expected to tend the kids. If he wants to go somewhere or do something, he does. If I want to, I have to do it in school hours or arrange a sitter. He will watch the boys, but I still have to work it out, just like a sitter. He seemed to forget that I was the one taking our son to school (NOT an easy task), doing the laundry, making sure the homework was done, and cooking meals. Guess he doesn't consider that work. School was where I needed the most help. He was refusing to go.*

There can, of course, be a number of different factors in the mix. As the following parent explains, it is not just what the couple is facing, but how they are facing it *together* that can make all the difference:

> *Autism is one of the most difficult disabilities to manage in a marriage, the main factor being TIME. When doing an applied behavior analysis program with my autistic children, eight hours were filled with just that. I home-school, and it is about a 10-hour a day job. I have to sleep with one of my autistic children because she does not sleep but about 5 hours a night and she will get up and wander. If I move, she wakes up! Not much nighttime romance there! Thank God, I have an understanding*

> *husband that knows if I did not give all this time to our children, they would not have made the progress they have made. It is a completely unselfish sacrifice. No wonder such a large number of couples with autistic children divorce.*

Truly, our sexuality as human beings is very much related to a host of other factors. Rarely does the issue stand in isolation. Another consideration that can powerfully influence our sexuality is our general health and the influence of any medications we are taking, or treatments we are receiving. While this is equally true for any couple, the issue may be especially relevant for those raising children with disabilities because of the frequency with which stress, anxiety, and depression may be involved. As one example:

> *In my case, I was and still am diagnosed as being clinically depressed. The drugs used to treat my depression had an effect on intimacy - they caused me to have less desire. Also, with my husband not accepting our sons' disability, or taking my hand and dealing with it together, we lost contact with each other's emotions very quickly.*

Even when the couple is well-connected to each other's emotions, their intimate moments may be colored by the needs of the child, and how they accommodate those requirements. A view of this sensitve subject of interruptions is as follows.

> *Sex is another fascinating issue as Bobby absolutely freaks about locked doors. Yup, we do manage to get some "locked door time" when he finally falls asleep in our bed and gets carried back to his bed for what hopefully is a full night's sleep. Woe to us, however, if Bobby does one of his nocturnal visits for reassurance when our bedroom door is locked. The last time that happened, I think the neighbors were ready to call 911 for an attempted murder or such at our house - thus was the decibel level of his pounding, screaming, and general hysteria. (Sex with one ear on the door is not a lot of fun for Mom and Dad, but it beats having the light turned on by Bobby as he runs into our room during the "wrong" time!)*

Sexual Self-Image

Yet another consideration that can have a strong bearing on sexuality is self-image. This far-reaching element of positive or negative thinking (and the feelings that go with it) can relate in part to how we see ourselves sexually and how we see our bodies. Some parents who have had a child with a disability may judge themselves as somehow defective. This is very much part of the blame game we discussed in Chapter 1. A perception of being sexually or reproductively inferior, or a belief that a child's disability is our punishment for sin, may become particularly pronounced in the bedroom. A parallel process can be involved as we look at our spouse. Our sexual attraction may be very much diminished if we think of our partner as sexually, reproductively or genetically inferior. Fears of having another disabled child may also weigh heavily if a couple is planning to have more children.

The solutions to such self-image problems are not different from what we have seen before. Raising self-awareness will be the first step, followed by a willingness and commitment to work this through, rather than to be ruled and limited by it. As always, effective communication will help raise the ability of the couple to resolve their troubled feelings and restore their mutual understanding and support. Professional help may be warranted if they are unable to resolve these issues on their own.

How Much Sex is Enough?

Another "none of my business" question I may have had to ask when doing counseling was how often the couple had sexual relations. Was it once a week, once a year, twice a day, Christmas and holidays ...? There was no right or wrong answer to this question—whatever they told me might be just fine. The key was always how *they* felt about it, whatever their answers were. If they said twice a year (or twice a day), and they were both very happy with that, who was I to tell them otherwise? However, it was very common that the numbers given were *not* mutually acceptable—that both parties were not equally happy with the frequency of their sexual activity. *This* was the issue that concerned me the most and would then become our point of departure. From here, we could begin to explore the issues and feelings involved, clear the air of resentments, talk about styles and preferences, explore the nature of any blocks or inhibitions, refer to specialists if necessary ... whatever would best help this couple move forward in whatever form was best for them.

There are a many books and educational videos that explore sexuality in great detail—not just the mechanics of "how to do it" but also the typically reported differences between men and women; the relationship of mind and emotions; the implications of past traumas, early learning, and parental role models; and so much more. Sex as sex is pretty straightforward, but sex as an aspect of a happy marriage has many aspects and intricacies. All are worthwhile, but it would take us far beyond our present purposes to delve into these many topics here.

Recommendations

The question of how couples can maintain a healthy level of sex, affection, and intimacy was not one of the questions specifically addressed at my meetings with parent support groups. It is easy to see, however, that with only minor adaptations, many of the recommendations made in earlier chapters will be equally relevant here:

1. **Communicate openly and honestly,** with love (not blame or anger). Build time to talk into your life together. Use "I" statements and a tone of caring.

2. **Share self-help materials,** such as books, articles, or educational videos about sexuality.

3. **Attend classes, workshops, or retreats** for marital enrichment— perhaps through community or church.

4. **Seek professional help if necessary.** Don't be afraid to ask for help.

5. **Commit to working together as a team** and to accepting shared responsibility.

6. **Set time every day or at least every week to talk** about how things are going; don't wait for a crisis to start talking.

7. **Be patient, and sensitive to the other partner's feelings** and priorities; ask them how best to approach them and when would be a good time to talk.

Chapter 9
Potentials

In this final chapter, I would like to share some of the thoughts that parents have shared with me about what has been most helpful to them. I have asked parents of children with disabilities, "What do you do when you feel troubled, sad or discouraged?" and, "What has helped you find peace with your child's disability and feel optimistic about the future?" There is little I can add to the clarity, wisdom, and purity of heart with which so many have replied.

Grief is such an important aspect of having a child with a disability. It never goes away and it's always with me. I am still learning to not let it overwhelm me or to cloud my judgments, but there are times, even now, when I really have to shove it to the back of my heart.

I found an anonymous quote once that said, "We must let go of the life we planned so as to accept the life that's waiting for us." In essence, that's what it's like to have a child with a disability. I had many hopes and plans for a "normal" child but that was not meant to be. Because of this, I had to let go of my hopes, my dreams, and accept the life that was waiting. And though there were times I felt like I had been cast into hell, I have learned since that I was really being led to a special place in life all along.

We haven't found peace with his autism. Far from it. We live on our nerves never knowing what he's going to do next, for example, cut through power cables, rip the taps off and flood the house ... We will never stop looking at so-called cures just in case, and we will never give up hope that one day he will return and speak to us. We only get discouraged when other people let us down, never with our son, and are sad when he is not at home.

He is in a 52-week-a-year school and we bring him home every other weekend. He has been at this school 5 years, and every time I take him back, it is just like the first time even though he likes it. It breaks our hearts, so we just get on with cleaning up the mess he's made. Later we start to smile at the things he's gotten up to while he's been home.

Everyone that has met us always asks, "But how do you manage to stay so happy? I wouldn't be able to cope!" We don't cope; we just wait until he returns to school then repair the house, and there is always a funny side to it. How many times have you heard, "We will look back and laugh at this one day"? This is what we do every week.

I find as Bobby gets older, I have more episodes of feeling sad about what he can't do. For example, I always had the vision of us taking him to Disney World and sharing that all-American vacation. Unfortunately, Bobby is TERRIFIED of "talking" puppets, figures, etc., not to mention completely overwhelmed by the sights, sounds, and stimulation that even a walk on Main Street in the Magic Kingdom produces. We tried twice, at different ages, to bring him and made it no further than the ticket booth. It's things like this, many on a much smaller scale, that leave me with fear for his future, along a with a sense of defeat at times. I try so hard to focus on what he CAN do, and the unique perspective that he brings to our world with his pinpoint humor and intelligence. Most of the time, rejoicing in the abilities that he has versus lingering with the "dis's" of his disability, saves me from the black hole of parental worry and despair, but oh, there are times I wish for the "fantasy land" of normalcy.

I have come to the conclusion that raising a child with a disability turns us parents into "heavy treaders." My husband and I are always treading onto the ground "where angels fear to go" to protect/advocate for our own precious angel. It's not an easy gait by any stretch either. We have been called thoughtless and uncaring of the rest of the world simply because our "treading" has to put our son first. My first reply to arrows of that sort is to ask the bearer, "If we don't speak out for Bobby, who will? Are you volunteering or just content criticizing US for being his voice?"

As for hope, it is a patchwork of discovery and avoidance. I allow hope to spring when I see Bobby latch onto a concept (like computers, animals, math, etc.) that could turn into a career for him as an adult. I avoid thoughts of his future on the larger scale most of the time as I take things "a day at time." I spend so much energy making sure that he has assistance navigating the everyday world, that I would get completely overwhelmed trying to work thoughts for the future into, "Now, how do I keep him from using the entire bottle of shampoo?"

I have hope that the decisions his father and I make now are going to bear the "fruit of acceptance" as Bobby goes out into the world himself someday. I hope that he will be accepted for who he is, no matter what special attributes he brings to his adult interactions, because of how his dad and I are teaching him to interact today.

The main way I keep my hopes up (and probably aggravate everyone around) is to look at where he was when he was three and how far he's come. At three, he was totally non-verbal, not potty trained, angry and AGGRESSIVE! Multiple hits and bites daily. Now look at him! Mainstream, but about a year or so behind, verbal, wanting friends, potty trained, able to navigate the school on his own, talks on the phone, etc. I feel this is because I wouldn't accept the 38 IQ the school said he had back at age three and kept pushing and fighting. I pulled him from the local self-contained preschool program and put him in a public preschool over our principal's LOUD screams. I held him back in kindergarten, again against the principal. I felt like if he was a year behind in speech and averaging a 62, let him repeat and be closer to the level of the other kids. Seems like it was good for him. He sure blossomed that year. I don't think his dad has accepted the label as well. Last he said was, "Hell, he's retarded, keep him home and quit torturing everyone." I can't go along with that.

I found peace almost right away about my sons' disabilities. I needed to accept their disabilities before I could fully educate myself on how to help them. Don't get me wrong, there was a quick mourning period of, "Oh, my God, will they ever live on their own, will they go to college, will they drive, will they marry and have children of their own?" I quickly got away from thinking like that and started taking one day at a time. I am very optimistic about their future. They are both making wonderful progress and participating in mainstream classes and activities at school. I also have talked with their doctors and they have told me that they them-selves have even gone to college with students that had mild autism. My sons' pediatrician went to medical school with a student with Asperger's, or high functioning autism, and he did extremely well. He had a therapeutic staff support worker with him to help keep him on task with a few things.

When I am feeling down the best thing I can do is to reach out to someone else in need. I can always find someone in worse shape than myself. If I reach out to someone or some cause, it always makes me feel better. If I don't have time to give, I can always write a small check. I make sure I always volunteer regularly in some way. Mostly I do this with our church. I love volunteering with children. Their comments and smiles when I teach them are so genuine. I love volunteering with the sick also. This helps me to forget about myself and feel better. I also believe talking with my friends and exercising help. When Arnie was very young, I would pray. I would ask for strength, calmness, and courage. Arnie is 27 now. I still ask for this guidance every day.

Parents often feel attacked by doctors, school personnel and protective services because the first thing they think is often that the parents are being abusive or neglecting their kids if a child has problems, or has scratches or bruises. So parents learn to get defensive and protective. But in time they find that it empowers them to develop good communication skills, to be clear about what is going on, and to be prepared to be accountable.

When I was in a mental fog, I would just go to my grandmother's home. I would just tell my husband that he'd have to deal with Brandon, that I had to have a break, and he was generally understanding about it.

My grandmother treated me like I was six years old, and I needed that. She cooked my favorite meals, let me sleep late, and nurtured me in ways that only grandmothers can. Usually a weekend was enough, because I'd start feeling guilty and would have thoughts of home.

To find peace with Brandon's disability, I just finally turned it over to God. I realized I couldn't "fix" him and it sure was going to take a higher power than what doctors offered. Once I turned it over to God, I then found contentment and acceptance. Plus, when I quit trying to change him into what I thought society thought he should be, well, only then, did I truly accept him for the wonderful person he really is. It was then that I began to truly see Brandon in the way that God intended him to be all along. I figured that if He could accept me, warts and all, then who was I not to accept Brandon? I had to accept that it was me that had to change - not him.

Looking back, I think I always kept a positive outlook because that's just my nature. Even in the worst of times, I would tell myself, "Well, it could be worse." I never, ever thought, "poor me" or "why me?" I always felt, "Why not me?"

My dear grandmother gave me the best words of advice, and they sustained me through rough times. She once said, "Honey, just keep one end fed and the other end dry, and he'll grow up just like everybody else." And you know what? My grandmother was right all along. Brandon did grow up just like everybody else.

The gifts we've received from Brandon have far outweighed the gifts we've given him. He gave us the gifts of tolerance, acceptance, patience, unconditional love, hope, and the best gift of all: faith.

Having an autistic child is one of the most powerful stressors a couple could ever face. If there are any weak points in the marriage, autism will weigh heavily upon them until they crack. A couple who might have spent a lifetime together quite happily can end up divorcing very quickly. And even the best marriages can get strained right up to the breaking point. However, for those that don't break, there can be a strengthening aspect: you get the attitude of "if we can survive this, then we can survive anything." Plus, the experience really brings home the idea that a couple has to be completely on the same side, in a struggle of us against the world, which is what all marriages should be but so rarely are.

In Conclusion

What is both interesting and significant is the degree to which the foregoing passages reflect a growing body of research findings. With remarkable consistency, those who have studied its impact on families report that having children with special needs does not have to be catastrophic. Quite the contrary. The evidence continues to mount suggesting that it can be a deeply enriching and even positively transformative process. I would like to share just a few inspiring summaries taken from the scientific community. They highlight the potentials that are offered by our children with special needs.

Research in the disability field is often dominated by studies of family stress, factors that affect stress, and ways of reducing stress for families. Many positive aspects were identified by the respondents. In summary parents mentioned the amount of patience, compassion, caring, strength and insight their child had taught them. Several mentioned how their child had taught them to just go on with life no matter what the problem is, and to face problems "head on." Also mentioned was the ability to assess situations and prioritize faster than previously, and learning how to deal with crisis more effectively than before. Others stated they had realized much sooner how valuable time spent with their children is. Also mentioned was an increased understanding and awareness of disabilities and appreciation of good health in other family members and not taking anything for granted. Particular rewards included knowledge that you had stepped up to and met the challenge given you.

Shriners Hospitals for Children

"Pathways for Transition Newspage"

Volume 4, September 28, 1999

www.shrinershq.org/choices/newspage4.html

All parents reported that the experience of raising a child with Down syndrome had a profound impact on their life. More importantly, they reported that the positive consequences associated with this experience far outweighed the negative ones. Positive consequences included: bringing the family closer together, learning the true meaning of unconditional love, putting things in proper perspective, and appreciating diversity.

Marcia Van Riper, Ohio State University

Reprinted from Down Syndrome Quarterly, March, 1999

www.denison.edu/collaborations/dsq/vanriper.html

Adoptive families of children with disabilities often comment that despite the undeniable challenges of parenting a child (or children) with disabilities or special adoption needs, the rewards outweigh the challenges. This comment is supported by research findings ... Many other studies of adoptive families of children with disabilities indicate findings of joy and satisfaction as well as benefits including: increased marital closeness; increased marital satisfaction; increased parental happiness; a positive impact on siblings; a closer, stronger family; greater patience, compassion and unselfishness; increased family cohesion; increased involvement in family, school and community; and, personal growth.

Institute on Human Development and Disability Update

Summer 2000

"Children of Choice - Adoptive/Foster Families Come in All Sizes, Shapes, and Colors"

www.uap.uga.edu/news00-choice.html

In spite of the unique demands of parenting a child with a disability, many parents have reported that, not only have they been able to manage their lives effectively, but they have also experienced beneficial outcomes related to parenting their children ... such as becoming more compassionate and self confident, making a difference for others, and gaining a more authentic view of what is valuable and important in life.

"Effective Life Management in Parents of Children with Disabilities:
A Survey Replication and Extension"
Lorraine Wilgosh, PhD, University of Alberta
Kate Scorgie, PhD, Azusa Pacific University
Darcy Fleming, MEd, University of Alberta
Developmental Disabilities Bulletin, Vol. 28 (2), 2000
www.ualberta.ca/~jpdasddc/ARTICLES/2000(2)/pp1-14Wilgoshetal

Recommendations

When asked what parents can do to restore their emotional balance when they feel sad, angry, overwhelmed, or another bad feeling, support group participants made the following recommendations:

1. *Find time alone to look at your feelings* and *to talk about them or resolve them in another way that works for you.*

2. *Explore the reasons for your feelings:* what leads you to feel that way, what triggered the feelings, what do you need from others?

3. *Partners must develop trust in each other and support one another.* They should encourage exploration of feelings and sharing them together, above all avoiding judgments.

4. *Self-awareness, and communication* with others who can be supportive and understanding.

5. *Find ways to relax,* even if it is only a walk around the block or reading a book.

6. *Seek professional help if necessary.*

7. *Read self-help books.*

8. *Find support groups* or other ways of networking.

9. *Use prayer.*

10. *Remember that "this too shall pass"—*having faith and keeping a perspective.

Appendix 1

A Six-Week Program for Couples

On the next few pages are six simple yet potentially powerful exercises. They are designed to help couples become more aware of themselves and each other, and to strengthen their ability to communicate effectively.

The exercises are designed to be easy and require very little time, perhaps 10-20 minutes each day. Try them for a week of five days each (or seven days if you prefer), and see how they work for you. You may find some of them to be not only worthwhile but actually fun, and you may want to continue some or all of them for longer than just a week.

There is an old saying that "what were once cobwebs are now cables." Like riding a bicycle, what may require a lot of careful attention in the beginning may soon become effortless and even second nature with just a little practice. As always, the purpose is to provide skills that may strengthen your partnering relationship. Try them and see if they do.

Contents

Week 1 ....Visioning Together

Week 2 ....Looking Together

Week 3 ....Working Together

Week 4...Learning Together

Week 5 ....Journaling Together

Week 6 ....Communicating Together

Week 1: Visioning Together

For a sailboat to reach its destination, it requires not only a good breeze but, just as importantly, a sense of direction. Similarly, for couples to accomplish great things, they must not only have a willingness to try, but they must also "set a direction" that will take them wherever it is they want to go. If our intention is to strengthen our partnering relationship, then we can set a course by establishing our goals and "holding the vision" of our success. A powerful technique for doing this is called a "paste-up." A paste-up is essentially a personalized poster that we make as a visual aid to help us become clear and focused on what we are trying to achieve.

Objective

To develop a shared vision of our partnership as we would ideally like to be, and to use that vision to help us move in the direction of our goals. [If we are a single parent, we can still use this exercise with great benefits as we clarify our *personal* directions—what we desire for ourselves.]

Materials

Poster paper, old magazines, colored markers, scissors, and glue

Technique

To be completed as time permits over the course of a week; schedule perhaps five 20-minute sessions with your partner [if single, then on your own]:

Make a List

of characteristics of the ideal parenting relationship that you would like to develop or strengthen for yourselves. The list might include such qualities as great listeners, understanding and supportive of each other, able to speak calmly even when seeing things differently, sharing household responsibilities, or any other characteristics you would choose for yourselves. Do this together with your partner, but limit your focus to the relationship and only list features that you both agree are important at this time (unless you are a single parent doing this paste-up only for yourself). Note that this technique can certainly be done again in the future when a different set of characteristics might be selected and agreed upon.

Find Your Symbols

Using old magazines, clip out words or pictures that represent the characteristics you have listed. For example, if I would like more time alone with my partner, I might clip out a picture of a couple having dinner by candlelight. I might also use the typed words, "Time Alone" or "Marriage Renewal," to verbally represent my goal. You can also use your own artistic abilities to sketch, paint, or stencil the words and pictures that represent your shared goals.

Make a Poster

Creatively arrange the words and pictures you have chosen, and glue them onto poster board to make a visual representation of your shared relationship goals.

Display Your Poster

of words and images where you will see it often, and remind yourself every day of what you are rapidly becoming!

Actively Use Your Poster

Spend a few minutes each day reviewing your poster, reaffirming your vision of success on a daily basis. Even if these are not yet fully true, tell yourselves such things as, "We are affectionate and kind to each other; we do find time to just relax and be together; we do listen attentively when the other one needs to share," or whatever your personal goals may be.

What we imagine we can do, we can do;
What we persistently imagine we can do, we cannot help doing.

Week 2: Looking Together

Objective

To raise our awareness of two critical issues in any parenting partnership: how we spend our time, and money.

Technique

Keep a Log

on two pages of a notebook for each day of the week. At lunch, dinner, and bedtime, take a moment to jot down how much time or money was spent and on what.

Share with your partner

on a daily basis what you are writing (share with a friend or family member if you don't have a partner). This sharing can be through discussion time or simply leaving your notebook where the other person can see it at a convenient time.

Notes: This exercise is not necessarily about change. Rather it is about raising our awareness so that we can be more conscious about our behavior in these very important areas. The idea is simply that:

With awareness comes the ability to make flexible choices.

Time		Money		
Noon	½ hour getting ready for work ½ hr driving to work 4 hrs working	gas		$20
6 p.m.	1 hr lunch 3 hrs working ½ hr driving home ½ hr shopping	lunch + tip candy juice and pop diapers batteries		$8 1 6 7 3

10 p.m.	½ hr dinner
	½ hr phone (answering messages)
	1 hr computer: e-mails /news
	½ hr paying bills
	½ hr fixing faucet
	1 hr relaxing with TV
		electric bill
		newspaper
		credit card:
		    gas (2x)
		    grocery
		    toys (presents)
		    hardware
			37
			72
			23
			16
				$73
				8
				
				148

Daily totals: Time:14 hrs accounted for; Money: $274.00

Week 3: Working Together

Objective

To improve our relationship by being very clear about what we would like from each other and making some short-term agreements:

Technique

Make a list

(separately) of up to 6 relatively little things you would like from your partner this week (taking out the trash without being asked would be a good example, while a Caribbean cruise would probably not be).

Revise your lists

by discussing them with your partner and crossing out items that cannot be freely and happily agreed upon at this time or cannot be easily accomplished this week. You may change the wording or add new items if necessary, so that your lists become comfortable for you both.

Make a commitment

that for one week you will do exactly what you have agreed. Make good on your promises and see how you fare. Chances are you'll see the nice boost to your relationship that often comes with such clarity of communication and willingness to respond to each other's requests.

Example

with cross-outs for what can not be freely agreed upon at this time. The lists don't have to involve the same number of items or the exact same time commitments (although they may). What is important is just that they represent what you both feel comfortable agreeing to for this one week. If you like how it works, you can always make a new list of agreements whenever you wish.

John's List	Mary's List
1. Make a nice dessert at dinner ~~twice~~ once this week.	1. Take out the garbage without being reminded.
2. Pick up the kids' toys in the living room before I get home from work.	2. Do the grocery shopping once if I give you a list.
3. Make sure I have enough clean shirts at the beginning of the week.	3. Fix the leaking faucet in the kitchen.
4. Be sure you have enough diapers so I don't have to go out at night.	4. ~~Refinish~~ Sand down Billy's dresser (just the top part).
5. Quit cooking with so much salt.	5. ~~Rake the leaves in the back yard~~.
6. Limit phone calls to ~~10~~ 20 minutes.	6. Watch the kids so I can have one hour to myself on Wednesday evenings.

Week 4: Learning Together

Make a Commitment

that, this week, you will each read a certain book or journal, or watch a personal growth video, and that you will both read or watch the same material. Be realistic and make sure that your agreement will not involve more time than you can comfortably arrange. Keep the focus on your relationship (not your children, investments or home improvements).

Agree on a Schedule

As an example: watch a self-help video borrowed from the library for 30 minutes a day on Monday and 30 minutes on Tuesday, and to talk about it for 20 minutes on Wednesday; then to read a journal article for 15 minutes on Thursday and discuss the article for 15 minutes on Friday.

Keep to the Agreements you have made.

One way you could approach this exercise might be to buy a copy of a best-selling self-help book for couples and agree to each read just one chapter. Maybe you'll decide you are most interested in the one having to do with developing similar styles of discipline, or maybe you are more interested in the chapter about rekindling a passionate romance. It doesn't matter, but unless you are both speed-readers with tons of extra time, a shorter commitment may have the greatest chance of success—just agree together to each read the same one chapter that interests you both.

Be flexible with how you schedule. It may work best for one partner to watch the video on two consecutive mornings, and the other partner to watch it all at once on a day off work. Another couple may be able to watch it together at the same time.

When you talk together about what you've watched or read, questions such as the following may help guide your discussion. Move in any way that you wish, as long as you stay on topic and are making good use of your valuable time.

1.	What were the main points we saw being raised by the book, video or article?
2.	What stands out as most valuable?
3.	If we were to act on one of those good suggestions, what would that look like—how would our relationship be different?
4.	Was there anything we disagreed with in the material? In what way? How might it have been better said?
5.	What do we have questions about? What might be a good topic for further exploration or study?

Week 5: Journaling Together

The process of journaling is simply one of making notes on a regular basis, so as to hold in focus whatever it is we may be trying to learn, create, or develop.

Objective

To strengthen our partnership by maintaining a high level of awareness, by keeping a daily journal of key observations, insights and experiences. [As with all of these exercises, if we are a single parent, we can still gain great benefits from doing these exercises on our own.]

Technique

Make a Commitment

to keep a daily journal of insights and observations that relate to your parenting partnership.

Keep a Journal

each day in whatever form works best for you. It could be at the end of the day just before bedtime, or first thing each morning after the kids have left for school. The journaling should be done separately, though you may choose to share at a time that is convenient for you (for example, after dinner each evening). Your notes should focus on the partnership and might include such things as: what you appreciated in your partner today; what concerns you may have had; any feelings that need to be aired and resolved; how you see your partnership progressing.

Continue through One Week

and then evaluate whether this exercise has been helpful and whether it is something you would like to continue.

Example of Journal Entries

Monday, 8:45 a.m. I find that I am a little nervous about writing my true feelings. I am afraid John will see me as too emotional or something. But I want him to know how important he is to me, and how much I want our marriage to remain strong.

10 a.m. Watched a TV show about teenagers and drugs and it really scared me. I wonder if John is also worried about the kids as they get older.

3 p.m. My friend, Mary, said she was going to visit her parents in Omaha. I wish we could find some time to travel once in a while. But with child care and bills to pay, I just don't see it. I wonder what the other parents do about this—will make a point to ask at our next support group meeting.

Week 6: Communicating Together

Objective

To improve our awareness and abilities in each of the four key areas of effective communication:

	1.	Hold a focus (one person and one issue at a time)
	2.	Talk from the heart (clearly express feelings and wants)
	3.	Listen with respect (like a sponge)
	4.	Maintain the spirit of friendship

Technique

Keep a log

each day this week, and give yourself a score on a scale of 1 to 10 (with 10 being perfect) for how well you did in each of these key areas. Add notes about any key observations or insights.

Example of Scoring (notes should also be included)

	Focus	Heart	Listen	Spirit	
Monday	6	7	4	8	
Notes:					
Tuesday	3	4	4	8	
Notes:					
Wednesday	7	7	9	10	
Notes:					
Thursday	9	5	7	10	
Notes:					
Friday	9	7	8	8	
Notes:					

Appendix 2
About Divorce

Divorce is such a huge topic. It brings together so many issues and could easily fill a book by itself; and there are many books already in print that are designed to offer support, encouragement, and practical guidance to those who are going through this major life change. Some of the many issues that are typically involved in the divorce process include preserving self-esteem, handling the changes in finances, supporting the children through such a major change, adjusting to being single again, and finding new relationships if one chooses. The list of the key aspects of divorce is, of course, much longer than these few, and it will vary with the particular couple and their individual circumstances—the reasons for their divorce, their extended family relationships, the number and ages of their children, their financial status, their personal strengths and coping skills, and so much more. We will focus here just briefly on the aspects of divorce that are particularly relevant, or even unique, to those raising children with disabilities.

Divorce: Same and Different

What are some of the ways in which couples facing divorce are most likely to have different experiences from the general population if they are raising children with disabilities? The obvious first answer may be just an intensification, perhaps an *extreme* intensification, of issues we have already discussed. Parents having difficulty finding child care may be losing an invaluable resource when one partner leaves the home. Parents already under pressure to find time may now have *more* pressure without the assistance of a partner. Parents struggling to meet the added expenses of a child's disabilities *may have* even less with which to meet those needs. Parents working hard to bring consistency and stability into their children's lives may suddenly be forced to help them through a challenging and perhaps unexpected period of inconsistency and instability. And yet, it is not always tragic or even difficult:

> *Surviving divorce for me was easy in the emotional aspect because my ex-husband was never "with me" to begin with. Me and the boys were no longer being abused. I took time after my marriage to find myself, and to also take more time to get further involved with my sons' needs, which I was unable to fully do when I was married because of him controlling me. I have found another relationship now, and he respects me and adores my sons. It took me time to accept even being treated by a man in an appropriate manner again. I was still walking on eggshells for a while, thinking I'd get beat if I made a salad a wrong way.*

Recommendations for Divorcing Couples

For anyone going through major changes, there will always be the challenge to think positively, conquer fear and doubt, and find effective ways to handle their "bad" feelings if and when they surface. These all-important topics were discussed in earlier chapters, especially those describing timelines, self-talk alternatives, and behavior trains (Chapters 1 and 6).

Parents attending support groups were asked what they thought would help couples move through divorce in the best way possible for themselves and their children. These were their suggestions:

1. **Focus on what's best for the children.** *Make a plan as to how both parents will continue to be involved and share parenting responsibilities.*

2. **Forgive your partner** *and get beyond your anger, for the benefit of the children.*

3. **Keep communications open** *despite the change in your relationship.*

4. **Avoid speaking ill of the other parent,** *no matter what you may secretly believe, and never fight with the other parent in front of the children.*

5. **Don't play one parent against the other** *or let the kids do that.*

6. **Don't use the children as an emotional football or weapon,** *or put them in the unhealthy and uncomfortable position of being between the parents. Children commonly draw conclusions that are not true, and often hold themselves responsible for the divorce—"If I had been more helpful, if it didn't cost so much to keep me ..." Don't fuel these fires.*

7. **Have faith, use prayer, and look for church or community support** *(such as singles groups or other support groups).*

8. **Seek counseling before a crisis.** *Make a plan; understand both what is and what will be involved for all members of the family.*

9. **Be sure that child support will be received:** *make a plan together; get a court order; cover yourself in terms of changes (future remarriage or a new girlfriend/boyfriend, or new responsibilities, or job changes, or a move ...).*

10. **Remember that both parents will always be important** *for the children, just as your children will always be important to you. Do whatever is necessary to maintain a positive relationship with the other parent, working together for the benefit of your children, or at least as "business partners" if it is not possible to remain as friends.*

Court Services and Minimizing Legal Costs

Couples can often avoid the high legal costs of a divorce by using mediation to develop a plan for the many issues involved—child support, custody (primary residence and decision-making authority), visitation (time sharing), division of property and debts, taxes, insurance and so on. This will save money, but also time, stress and bitterness. It will also keep the parents "in the driver's seat" in that the couple will be the ones making the decisions about their family, rather than having the decisions made for them by a judge. Some of these topics can also be addressed in counseling, such as how the parents will remain active and involved with the children, which parent could provide the better primary home for the children, and what visitation schedule would work best for them.

Mediation services are often available at reduced or no cost, and the local courthouse and phone book are good places to start looking for what is available. Some courts offer classes, forms and assistance to couples doing their divorce without attorneys, and there are also self-help divorce books and do-it-yourself packets available at libraries and bookstores. Another option is to look to attorneys for legal advice and the filing of formal documents, while doing as much of the preparatory work as possible on their own, perhaps with the help of a mediator. Another service being provided through some courts is parent education classes for divorcing couples; attendance is even mandatory in some jurisdictions.

Beginning Anew

Of course, not everyone who is divorced is in any hurry to start a new relationship. Some may be very comfortable to remain single and unattached. Others have found a comfortable middle ground:

> *I am an always single parent - never married. I have found life online to be my lifesaver. I have met several very important people to my son's and my life online. I find that getting to know someone online has allowed a person I might be interested in to get to know me and my child, without them risking getting too involved before they know they can handle a disabled child in their life, and before my child gets to know them and care about them. I also find that having an online relationship with someone with only periodic face-to-face involvement allows me to keep my son's needs foremost the majority of the time—but allow me to take a break periodically to spend time with an adult. I also find that the adults I become involved with can handle having my son in their life on a part-time basis, but could not on a full-time basis. I know most people want more than a part-time relationship, but I have actually come to prefer "part-time physical/full-time emotional" relationships.*

Who Would Ever Want Me?

One challenge for those desiring to start new relationships has to do with the perception that dating is necessarily more difficult when children have disabilities:

> *Many people, my close friends included, had this saying, "Well, there will not be many guys who would want to marry a mother with three children and one autistic." It hurts to hear people making judgments just like that. The key here was not to care about preconceived ideas and to search for real love. I did find real love and am happily married for two years now.*

Indeed, many parents of children with disabilities have found new and fulfilling relationships. The fact of a disability is never as much of an obstacle as the beliefs we hold about it. Believing that it IS possible to find Mr. or Mrs. Right can be powerful (just as disbelief and negative thinking can be so very limiting).

One parent made the following suggestions for those who want to start anew:

I think for anyone beginning a new relationship, especially with disabled children, you want to make sure that the new person in your life understands what needs your kids have, and the time that you invest in them and will continue to invest in them. With me it was a win/win situation. My boyfriend helped me get them out in the community, which I was unable to do too much on my own because of some of their behaviors, which were too much to handle for one person. I found out that they loved nature and loved being out with him. He taught them how to fish, race remote control cars, play baseball and football. Basically he has taken on the DAD role here.

Recommendations from Support Groups

Parents attending support group meetings were asked what recommendations they would offer to divorced parents of children with disabilities who want to start dating or find a new partner. These were their suggestions:

1. *Join a church or singles group*, or get involved in Special Olympics as a way of meeting new people.

2. *Look for a partner with a caring attitude*, not a handsome face. If the partner cannot accept you because of your child, know that from the beginning. Don't set yourself up for surprises by hiding it.

3. *Help the newcomer know what to expect.* Be honest about the nature of the disability and dispel myths about bad genes, contagious conditions, and similar misunderstandings.

4. *Be a unified team:* don't undermine the newcomer's authority, but support them to develop their own relationship with the child.

5. *Be realistic and know that it will take time* for the newcomer to form a relationship with the child.

6. *Talk openly* about parenting styles, values, etc. Get premarital counseling before remarriage.

7. *Ask if they will be willing to attend educational programs and support groups with you.* Look for someone who is willing to be involved with your child.

8. *Don't involve your children until the relationship is "for real,"* because it can be hard for children to have different parent figures coming and going in their lives.

Appendix 3

3-1: A Workshop for Support Groups

Modern educators understand that people usually gain very little from what they hear but gain a great deal from what they say or do. For this reason, there has been a movement away from lecture and demonstration as training approaches, and instead towards getting the group actively involved—talking, sharing, solving problems together, doing role plays and so on. Part of this "experiential approach to learning" involves the use of structured exercises to promote group participation.

Much of the material and many of the recommendations made in this book came from parents who participated in two very simple structured exercises. These served as springboards for discussion and are presented on the following pages: "A Marriage and Relationships Survey" and a "Marriage and Relationships Exercise." It might be worthwhile to outline the steps by which these can be used in a workshop format. Some readers may wish to recommend such activities for their own parent support groups. Not only are the exercises fun, but the group discussion that follows from them can be extremely valuable in providing helpful suggestions and highlighting community resources. The two exercises are also presented in Spanish (Appendix 3-4 and 3-5).

As a time frame, 1.5 to 2 hours is recommended. This time can be divided as follows:

Workshop Agenda

1. **Introductions (10 minutes)**

2. **Stage Setting (5 minutes)**

3. **Survey Exercise (10 minutes)**

4. **Compilation (15 minutes)**

5. **Group Discussion (as time permits)**

6. **Break (10 minutes)**

7. **Small Group Exercise (15 minutes)**

8. **FULL Group Discussion (as time permits)**

9. **Closing REMARKS**

Introductions

All participants should have a chance to introduce themselves, perhaps with their names, number and ages of children, and anything else they might like to share. It may be helpful to have them make name tags or paper name tents so that they can interact on a more personalized level during the program.

Stage Setting

The workshop agenda should be posted or circulated so that everyone knows the schedule and how they are progressing in terms of the available time. Pointing out where the restrooms are, having snacks and drinks available, announcing that there will be a break after the first hour ... all of these help to assure that the program will run more smoothly. You might suggest that people turn off their cell phones, unless it is really necessary to keep them on. Another recommendation is to ask for agreement that anything shared of a personal nature will be kept confidential and not repeated.

Survey Exercise

Circulate copies of the "Marriage and Relationships Survey" (Appendix 3-2). Ask each participant to complete it to the best of their ability, but only if they are the parent or guardian of a child with a disability. If both partners are present, they can each fill one out. Be sure to tell the participants not to put their names on it, because the survey will be anonymous—no one will know who has written what. Once the group has finished, collect the surveys, shuffle them well, and then return them to the group so that each person has a completed survey form, but not their own.

With a blackboard or flip chart handy, ask the participants to share what they see on the survey paper they received, starting with question #1 about time alone by yourself or with your partner—"How many had no answer at all (left blank)? How many have a '0' circled? How many have a '1'?" and so on, one by one, all the way to number "10." As the group gives their responses, write the numbers on the board or flip chart so that the group can see how they did *as a group*. Then move on and do the same with survey question #2. A group profile will emerge that looks something like the example shown on the following chart entitled, "Survey Compilation."

Survey Compilation
(example, assuming 20 participants)

Blank	0	1	2	3	4	5	6	7	8	9	10
Question 1: Time Alone											
1	3	2	0	2	1	3	3	0	2	2	1
Question 2: Help With Child Care											
2	1	0	4	4	2	3	3	0	2	0	0
Question 3: Meeting Extra Expenses											
0	3	2	0	2	1	4	3	0	2	2	1
Question 4: Shared Approach to Discipline											
0	1	2	3	2	1	3	3	0	1	3	1
Question 5: Satisfying Love Life											
1	3	2	0	2	1	3	3	0	2	2	1
Question 6: Resources for Guidance											
0	2	2	0	2	1	3	5	0	2	2	1
Question 7: Partners Talk Openly											
1	3	2	0	2	1	6	3	0	2	0	0
Question 8: Resolve Bad Feelings Quickly											
0	0	0	0	2	1	5	5	3	1	2	1
Question 9: Share Responsibilities Comfortably											
1	3	2	0	2	1	3	3	0	2	2	1
Question 10: Optimistic About Future											
0	0	0	1	1	1	4	4	3	2	1	4

Conclude this segment of the workshop by asking such questions as, "Where do our scores seem highest? Why do you think that is? What scores are lowest? Any ideas about that? Are there any areas of concern that were not covered in this survey? How did you like this exercise? Any other insights or thoughts?" These and similar questions should stimulate some lively discussion, but watch the time so that you can break at the end of the first hour (or however much time has been allocated for the first half of the program).

> **Notes:**
>
> *When 88 parents from seven different support groups were given this survey, their scores averaged roughly 4 to 6 for all ten questions. What was particularly interesting, however, was that there was a very broad spread of scores, with about as many lows as highs, rather than most being in the middle. This fits well with the point made in the Introduction that "disabilities" is a category term that represents enormous variation, both among the children and among their parents.*

Break

This next segment of the workshop may seem so self-evident as to warrant no comment. After all, what could be more obvious than taking a break after about an hour? Still, it is worth emphasizing how important it is that the group be given a leg stretch, an opportunity to visit the restroom, and a chance to digest all that has been covered. Breaks are important for a number of reasons, and without them, the quality of learning and the level of enjoyment usually goes downhill. The same is true for providing snacks and drinks. Not only are they a nice way to welcome the group members, but they also assure that learning will not suffer as a result of people feeling hungry, thirsty or just plain disappointed.

Small Group Exercise

The next segment begins by dividing the group into smaller units of perhaps three to five at a table. The exact number is not so important and will depend on how many participants are present. Once organized into smaller groups, each group is assigned one, two, or three of the questions from the "Marriage and Relationships Exercise" that follows (Appendix 3-3). If it is a large gathering of, say, 40 people, ten groups can be formed and each group assigned one of the questions. On the other hand, if it is a meeting of perhaps 17, then perhaps they can be divided into three groups of three people and two groups of four, with each of these five subgroups assigned two of the exercise questions.

Suggest that each small group appoint a spokesperson to take notes and report back to the full group at the end of the exercise. Allow plenty of time for discussion among the small groups, but check in every so often to make sure they are on task and likely to finish in a total of 15-20 minutes.

Full Group Discussion

Return to a full group focus and have each spokesperson report on the recommendations made by their subgroup. You might want to record the suggestions so that copies can be typed up later for those who were present, as well as for those who were not. Another option might be to post the suggestions at a group website or circulate them through a newsletter or mailing.

Closing Remarks

A few minutes can be saved at the end of the meeting to "bring closure" to the program by giving the participants a chance to share anything they would like to add. This short but important segment can be facilitated with such questions as, "How did you all feel about our workshop tonight? Any suggestions as to how we can best follow up with the information shared? Before we close for this evening, is there anything anyone would like to say?" Of course, this is also a good time to touch upon other issues, such as any general announcements and the dates and topics of your upcoming meetings.

Appendix 3-2
A Marriage and Relationships Survey

Circle the number that shows how much you agree or disagree with each statement. If you are not in a relationship now, answer in terms of when you were in a parenting partnership or marriage. Leave blank if not applicable.

strongly disagree	somewhat disagree	somewhat agree	strongly agree

1) I can usually find time alone with my partner or by myself when I feel a need for it.

0   1   2   3   4   5   6   7   8   9   10

2) I have a variety of sources I can look to for help with child care.

0   1   2   3   4   5   6   7   8   9   10

3) I have been able to meet the extra expenses of my child's disability without trouble.

0   1   2   3   4   5   6   7   8   9   10

4) My partner and I share a similar approach to child rearing and discipline.

0   1   2   3   4   5   6   7   8   9   10

5) Our love life (sex, affection, and intimacy) has remained healthy and satisfying.

0   1   2   3   4   5   6   7   8   9   10

strongly disagree	somewhat disagree	somewhat agree	strongly agree

6) I have lots of people to turn to for guidance, information, support and encouragement.

0   1   2   3   4   5   6   7   8   9   10

7) My partner and I talk together openly about our feelings, challenges and concerns.

0   1   2   3   4   5   6   7   8   9   10

8) When I feel sad or unhappy, I know how to move through it fairly quickly.

0   1   2   3   4   5   6   7   8   9   10

9) My partner and I are happy with the way we share family and child care responsibilities.

0   1   2   3   4   5   6   7   8   9   10

10) We have found peace with our child's disability and are optimistic about the future.

0   1   2   3   4   5   6   7   8   9   10

Appendix 3-3
A Marriage and Relationships Exercise

1. **Parents complain that finding time alone with their partner**, or just to be by themselves, can be very hard to do. What suggestions can we make?

2. **Parents often approach child rearing and discipline very differently.** How can they work together as a unified team?

3. **Parents of children with special needs often feel alone with their many feelings.** Where can they go for guidance, information, and support?

4. **Parents often play the genetic "blame game,"** and see the other partner at fault when they discover that their child has a disability. How can they move beyond this unhelpful process?

5. **Feeling bad at times is normal, and yet learning how to resolve bad feelings is important.** What can parents do to restore their emotional balance when they feel sad, angry, overwhelmed, or another bad feeling?

6. **It can be hard to get competent and affordable child care,** especially when a child's disabilities are severe. What avenues are open to parents?

7. **Special needs often involve extra financial expenses** that are not covered by insurance. What can help parents manage the extra expense of a child's disabilities, such as testing, office visits, child care, co-pays, etc.?

8. **Communication between couples is often the key** to supporting each other and resolving differences. How can couples communicate most effectively?

9. **If a couple has decided to divorce** (whatever the reasons), what would help them move through it in the best way possible for them selves and their children?

10. **Imagine a single parent of a child with a severe disability that wants to start dating and find a new partner.** What recommendations can we give?

Appendix 3-4
Encuesta de Matrimonio y Relaciones

Ponga un circulo en el numero que indica si esta de acuerdo o desacuerdo con cada descripcion. Si usted no tiene ninguna relacion ahora, conteste como cuando usted estaba casado(a) o tenia una pareja. Si no le aplica, no lo circule.

gran desacuerdo   poco desacuerdo   de acuerdo   muy de acuerdo

1) Usualmente puedo encontrar tiempo para mi o con mi pareja cuando siento que lo necesito.

0   1   2   3   4   5   6   7   8   9   10

2) Yo tengo una variedad de recursos que me pueden ayudar con cuidado de niños.

0   1   2   3   4   5   6   7   8   9   10

3) Yo he podido pagar los gastos extras de mi hijo(a) con desabilidad sin problemas.

0   1   2   3   4   5   6   7   8   9   10

4) Mi pareja y yo compartimos ideas similares sobre crianza y diciplina del niño(a).

0   1   2   3   4   5   6   7   8   9   10

5) Nuestra vida amorosa (sexo, afecto, y intimidad) continua saludable y satisfactoria.

0   1   2   3   4   5   6   7   8   9   10

gran desacuerdo   poco desacuerdo   de acuerdo   muy de acuerdo

6) Conozco muchas personas que pueden guiarme y darme apoyo, informacion, y animo.

0   1   2   3   4   5   6   7   8   9   10

7) Mi pareja y yo somos francos sobre nuestros sentimientos, retos, y preocupaciones.

0   1   2   3   4   5   6   7   8   9   10

8) Cuando me siento triste o infeliz, se como sobreponerme con facilidad.

0   1   2   3   4   5   6   7   8   9   10

9) Mi pareja y yo somos felices con la manera que compartimos las responsibilidades y e cuidado de la familia.

0   1   2   3   4   5   6   7   8   9   10

10) Nosotros hemos encontrado paz con la desabilidad de nuestro hijo(a) y somos opti- mistas sobre el futuro.

0   1   2   3   4   5   6   7   8   9   10

Appendix 3-5
Ejercicios de Matrimonio y Relaciones

1. **Padres se quejan de que no encuentran tiempo para su pareja,** o para ellos mismos, y que es muy dificil de hacer. Que sugerencias podemos dar?

2. **Frecuentemente, los padres crian y diciplinan muy diferente.** Como pueden lograr hacerlo de una manera unida como un equipo?

3. **Padres de niños con necesidades especiales se sienten solos con sus sentimientos.** A donde pueden acudir para guia, informacion, y apoyo?

4. **Padres caen en "el juego de la culpa"** y culpan al otro cuando des cubren que su hijo(a) tiene alguna desabilidad. Como se pueden ellos mover de esta etapa que no les ayuda?

5. **Sentirse mal a veces es normal, y aprender como resolver estos sentimientos es importante.** Que pueden hacer los padres para restaurar su balance emocional cuando se sienten tristes, enojados, sobrecargados, o tengan otro mal sentimiento?

6. **Puede ser dificil encontrar cuidado competente y razonable,** espe cialmente cuando las desabilidades del niño(a) son severas. Que avenidas estan disponibles a los padres?

7. **Necesidades especiales involucra gastos financieros extras** que no son cubridos por aseguranza. Que puede ayudar a los padres a costear los gastos extras del niño(a) con desabilidades con visitas de doctor, examenes, cuidado, pagos, etc.?

8. **Communicacion entre parejas es la llave** para apoyarse mutua mente y resolver diferencias. Como se pueden las parejas comu nicar de una manera mas efectiva?

9.   **Si las parejas han decidido divorciarse** (cualquiera sea la razon), que les ayudaria a seguir en la mejor direccion posible por ellos mis mos y sus hijos?

10. **Imagine un padre/madre soltero(a) con un niño(a) con desabilidad severa.** Si el/ella quiere empazar a salir y encontrar una nueva pareja, que recomendaciones le puede dar?